THE MAGIC TRIVIA BOOK

An entertaining collection of
1,000 Rock 'N' Roll
Trivia Questions

George and Paul Buchheit

The Magnificent Music Trivia Book

An entertaining collection of
1,000 Rock 'N' Roll trivia questions,
from the 50's to the 90's

2nd Edition
Copyright 2003, 2010 George and Paul Buchheit
All rights reserved.

No part of this book may be reproduced, stored in a retrieval system, or transmitted by any means, electronic, mechanical, photocopying, recording, or otherwise, without written permission from the authors.

Cover art and illustration by Darren Blakely.

Occasional references are made to a listing of all-time Rock 'N' Roll songs. These are references to Joel Whitburn's The Billboard Book of Top 40 Hits (Billboard Publications, 1992)

Dedication:

To Andrea, Gary, Amorn, Joe, and Marisa

We welcome comments about our book. Please email us at
TriviaRnR@aol.com

-- George & Paul

Forward

If you're reading this, you most likely have an interest in Rock 'N' Roll, trivia, or both. This book is meant to provide some entertainment to the many people who like music, enjoy some trivia and don't mind learning a little something along the way. **The Magnificent Music Trivia Book** is a well-researched, Internet-tested collection of trivia questions based on the songs of the 50s, 60s, 70s, 80s and 90s. There's a little bit of musical memory for everyone. Each question includes the percentage of people who answered correctly when these questions were originally posed on the Internet.

The Internet Connection

All of the questions found inside this book were first developed and used as part of the original "Baby Boomer Music Trivia" site on the Internet. The game was played on a weekly basis by thousands of people. Their enthusiastic participation allowed us to maintain files on the difficulty levels of all of the questions, which allows you to compare your success rate with others who have an interest in music trivia. Difficulty levels range from questions answered correctly by up to 99% of our players to questions which challenge even the most knowledgeable song lovers. You can decide how to use this feature, whether you're playing solo, with a group, or going head-to-head with a music trivia rival. It's very easy to tell how your trivia expertise compares with other players.

Table of Contents

Chapter 1 - The 50s and the Early 60s

GAME 1 - ELVIS AND THE EARLY ROCKERS   Page 3

GAME 2 - FLOATIN' THROUGH THE 50s   Page 8

GAME 3 - WHO SANG THESE? (50s/60s)   Page 13

GAME 4 - SUBTITLES FROM THE 50s/60s   Page 18

GAME 5 - SAILIN' THROUGH THE 60s   Page 23

GAME 6 - SARCASTIC 60s   Page 28

GAME 7 - MORE SARCASTIC 60s   Page 34

GAME 8 - WHO SANG THESE? (60s)   Page 39

GAME 9 - THE TRICKY 60s   Page 44

GAME 10 - THE PSYCHEDELIC 60s   Page 50

Chapter 2 - From the 60s to the 70s

GAME 1 - LYRICAL BITS FROM THE 60s AND 70s   Page 57

GAME 2 - 70s WHO - WHAT - WHERE   Page 62

GAME 3 - BITS & PIECES FROM THE 60s AND 70s   Page 67

GAME 4 - BEATLES I	Page 72
GAME 5 - BEATLES II	Page 76
GAME 6 - 60s SOUL	Page 80
GAME 7 - TOUGH SOUL (60s/70s)	Page 85
GAME 8 - QUICKIES FROM THE 60s AND 70s	Page 90
GAME 9 - WHO-WHAT-WHERE IN THE 60s AND 70s	Page 94
GAME 10 - MORE QUICKIES FROM THE 60s & 70s	Page 98

Chapter 3 - The 70s

GAME 1 - SLIPPIN' THROUGH THE 70s	Page 105
GAME 2 - WHO SANG THESE? (70s)	Page 110
GAME 3 - FLASHBACKS FROM THE 70s	Page 115
GAME 4 - SLIDIN' THROUGH THE 70s	Page 120
GAME 5 - 70s SONG THEMES	Page 125
GAME 6 - MORE 70s SONG THEMES	Page 130
GAME 7 - SUBTITLES FROM THE 70s	Page 135
GAME 8 - WHAT 70s SONG WAS THAT?	Page 140
GAME 9 - 70s VARIETY	Page 145
GAME 10 - THE SNEAKY 70s	Page 150

Chapter 4 - The 80s and the 90s

GAME 1 - 80s SONG THEMES   Page 157

GAME 2 - EASY 80s   Page 162

GAME 3 - MATCH THE LYRICS With The 80s SONG   Page 167

GAME 4 - WHO SANG THESE? (80s)   Page 171

GAME 5 - EYEING THE 80s   Page 176

GAME 6 - MORE 80s   Page 181

GAME 7 - EASIN' THROUGH THE 80s   Page 186

GAME 8 - FLASHBACKS FROM THE 80s   Page 191

GAME 9 - SUBTITLES FROM THE 80s/90s   Page 196

GAME 10 - NAVIGATING THROUGH THE 90s   Page 201

Chapter 5 - Potpourri

GAME 1 - MEMORABLE QUOTES   Page 209

GAME 2 - SILLY SONGS   Page 213

GAME 3 - Pretitles THROUGH THE YEARS   Page 218

GAME 4 - ONE-HIT WONDERS   Page 223

GAME 5 - JAMMIN' WITH THE JACKSONS   Page 228

GAME 6 - THE BRITISH INVASION   Page 233

GAME 7 - GUYS AND GALS   Page 238

GAME 8 - MORE GUYS AND GALS   Page 243

GAME 9 - FIND THE PHONY (60s)   Page 248

GAME 10 - FIND THE PHONY (70s/80s)   Page 253

Answers

Chapter 1 - The 50s and the Early 60s   **Page 261**
Chapter 2 - From the 60s to the 70s   **Page 261**
Chapter 3 - The 70s   **Page 262**
Chapter 4 - The 80s and the 90s   **Page 263**
Chapter 5 - Potpourri   **Page 264**

Chapter 1 - The 50s and the Early 60s

GAME 1 - ELVIS AND THE EARLY ROCKERS

Time to get in the "way-back machine." Read the clues and make your choice...

1. Elvis had his first No. 1 in 1956, HEARTBREAK HOTEL, which was on the charts for 22 weeks and at the top for 8! It's always crowded at this place for broken-hearted lovers, but you can still find some room. Where was it located.....?
   A Highway 6
   B Lonely Street
   C Tupelo
   D next to the River of Tears   {95% correct on the Internet}

2. In August of 1956, HOUND DOG was released, on the flip side of Don't Be Cruel. This record was No. 1 for 11 weeks! Well, that Hound Dog "never caught a rabbit" and, according to the lyrics, what did "they" say about her (it?).....?
   A "you're the cats"
   B "up your nose with a rubber hose"
   C "you were alright"
   D "you was high-classed"   {94% correct on the Internet}

3. The flip side, DON'T BE CRUEL, helped make this Elvis' biggest seller ever and one of the most popular rock singles ever. Although not always shown, this song had a subtitle, which was.....?
   A (To A Heart That's True)
   B (I'm No Fool)
   C (There Is A Time)
   D (It's Now Or Never)   {96% correct on the Internet}

4. Listed as Elvis' third biggest seller, ALL SHOOK UP was No. 1 for nine weeks in 1957. By now, he was already the "King" of pop music (and endorsements). At the beginning of this song, what did he say he was "itching like".....?
   A a trigger finger on the old roscoe
   B a man with allergic eczema
   C a man on a fuzzy tree
   D a dog with fleas   {67% correct on the Internet}

3

5. In June of 1957, (LET ME BE YOUR) TEDDY BEAR debuted. Only about one minute and 45 seconds long, this song has been listed as one of the top 50 rock songs of all time. In this song, which two animals did Elvis say he didn't want to be.....?
   A loaded goat and lake loon
   B polar bear and grizzly bear
   C tiger and lion
   D alligator and crocodile   {81% correct on the Internet}

6. It didn't take Elvis long to have another smash. In October of 1957, JAILHOUSE ROCK stayed on the charts for almost five months. Lots of trivia in this song. For instance, which group was "the whole rhythm section".....?
   A Able, Baker and Charlie
   B The Five Miscounts
   C the Brady boys
   D the Purple Gang   {73% correct on the Internet}

7. We can't resist.....there are too many good questions in JAILHOUSE ROCK. In verse four, who was "a-sittin' on a block of stone". (Hint: he's the one the warden told not to be square, "if you can't find a partner, use a wooden chair!").....
   A Johnny Rotten
   B Hodie Snitch
   C the sad sack
   D lazy bones   {54% correct on the Internet}

8. Can you put up with just one more from JAILHOUSE ROCK? In verse five, Shifty Henry told Bugs that this was their chance to make a break. But Bugsy wanted to stick around a while and get his kicks. What was his negative response to Shifty.....?
   A nix, nix
   B that won't click
   C no tricks
   D nip it (in the bud)   {64% correct on the Internet}

9. In 1960, Elvis made it to No. 1 with STUCK ON YOU, which was the his first post-Army single. It is listed as high as No. 8 for the year.

So, Elvis says that once he catches his girl and the kissing starts.....?
  A "he couldn't find a camel in a shopping cart"
  B "a team of wild horses couldn't tear us apart"
  C "kerosene cucumbers couldn't burn my heart"
  D "the arrow of love finds his heart"   {84% correct on the Internet}

10. Last Elvis question for this game. In 1961, he made it to No. 1 with GOOD LUCK CHARM. In this song he mentions a four-leaf clover, an old horseshoe, a rabbit's foot and a silver dollar. But what does he say he would do if he found a lucky penny.....?
  A toss it across the bay
  B throw it at a freshman
  C throw it in Kelsey's Ocean
  D skip it over the lake   {59% correct on the Internet}

11. In 1955, Bill Haley & His Comets hit it big with the classic (WE'RE GONNA) ROCK AROUND THE CLOCK. It has been listed as one of the top ten rock and roll songs of all time. At the beginning of the song, what does the singer tell "hon" to put on.....?
  A her high-heel sneakers
  B her gardenia blossom perfume
  C her glad rags
  D her poodle skirt   {51% correct on the Internet}

12. Also in 1955, Chuck Berry, the very influential early rocker, first hit the charts with a song about MAYBELLENE. Chuck wants her to be true and, while out driving, ends up in a "car chase" with her. What kind of car was Maybellene driving.....?
  A hotrod Lincoln
  B Hudson Terraplane
  C nifty Fifty
  D Cadillac Coupe DeVille   {73% correct on the Internet}

13. In 1957, Berry had his second big hit with a song called SCHOOL DAY. It's all about teenagers dealing with school and what happens after 3:00, when the school day ends. At the very beginning of the song, what does Chuck say the teacher is teaching.....?

A the Emancipation Proclamation
  B the golden rule
  C not much
  D Science   {88% correct on the Internet}

14. In late 1957, Charles Berry had his next big hit, ROCK & ROLL MUSIC, which was later done by the Beatles. When he says "I have no kick against" a certain kind of music, "unless they try to play it too darn fast", he referred to......?
  A Latin rhythms
  B hesitation waltz
  C marching music
  D modern jazz   {82% correct on the Internet}

15. In 1956, Carl Perkins was on the chart for four months with BLUE SUEDE SHOES. It might have been No. 1, but it was released the same day as Elvis' Heartbreak Hotel. Finish the opening line, "one for the money, two for the show, three to get ready....."?
  A "Larry, Curly, Moe"
  B "now go, cat, go"
  C "and four to go"
  D "it's time to blow"   {96% correct on the Internet}

16. How about one from Jerry Lee Lewis? In 1957, "The Killer" spent almost five months on the charts with WHOLE LOT OF SHAKIN' GOING ON. Based on the references in the song, where is the "shakin'" most likely happening.....?
  A Robert E. Lee Natural Bridge
  B on a farm
  C up on the roof
  D in the firehouse   {50% correct on the Internet}

17. 1958 saw Jerry (And His Pumping Piano) again hit it big, this time with GREAT BALLS OF FIRE, a high-energy song if there ever was one! In this classic, Jerry tells us what too much love does to a man.....
  A drives him insane
  B turns him into possum pie
  C makes him say, "ebum, shubum, shubum, shubum"
  D makes him dizzy   {96% correct on the Internet}

18. In 1958, Danny & The Juniors had a classic called AT THE HOP, which stayed at No.1 for seven weeks! Apparently, the song was first titled "Do The Bop". In this song, what terms are used to refer to the song's young swingers.....?
  A guys and dolls
  B dudes and dudettes
  C cats and chicks
  D Charlene and Dud   {70% correct on the Internet}

19. In 1957, Little Richard, born Richard Wayne Penniman, had one of his biggest hits with a song called KEEP A KNOCKIN'. In this song, what does Richard repeatedly tell "the knocker" after telling her she can't come in.....?
  A "how do you do, Mrs. Wiley?"
  B "don't ever let me see you again"
  C "come back tomorrow night and try it again"
  D "see you later, alligator"   {65% correct on the Internet}

20. The last question is about Fats Domino and one of his many big hits of the late 50s, called BLUEBERRY HILL. On that famous night when "the moon stood still", what did the "wind in the willow" play.....?
  A an unchained melody
  B "Boil That Cabbage Down"
  C love's sweet melody
  D the song in our hearts   {85% correct on the Internet}

GAME 2 - FLOATIN' THROUGH THE 50s

Be careful.....songs from the 50s can be tough, even these big hits.

1. This was a top ten song from 1956. The artist was Jim Lowe, who was a New York City DJ (rival stations in NY refused to play the hit!). He wanted to get into a swingin' night spot, but there was an obstacle which was keeping a secret.....
   A Dark Moon
   B Ivory Tower
   C The Green Door
   D Poison Ivy   {69% correct on the Internet}

2. Another 1956 top 10-er. Johnny Ray remade this song, originally done by a group of inmates at a Tennessee prison (for real). Johnny is quite sad, thinking about his lost love and "tryin' to forget". People stare and call him a fool, because he is.....
   A Just Walking In The Rain
   B Standing On The Corner
   C The Happy Whistler
   D On The Street Where You Live   {70% correct on the Internet}

3. Gogi Grant had the highest-ranking female vocal of 1956. It had a western style and was immensely popular, holding at No. 1 for as many as eight weeks. It was about a guy who "yearned to wander" and he was called.....
   A (The) Canadian Sunset
   B The Wayward Wind
   C The Great Pretender
   D The Happy Whistler   {67% correct on the Internet}

4. On to The King, let's go to him now (wherever he may be). This song was Elvis' first big hit. It was a "smash", also staying at No.1 for eight weeks. It's about where you go if your baby leaves you, this place at the end of Lonely Street.....
   A Heartbreak Hotel
   B Blueberry Hill
   C Hotel California
   D Waterloo   {99% correct on the Internet}

5. Last one from 1956 was by Guy Mitchell and ranked as high as No. 2 for the year. It stayed at the top of the charts for ten weeks! It's about a lost love (wow, there are a lot of those!). The dream is gone, he has lost her and he feels like crying all night.....
  A Whatever Will Be, Will Be (Que Sera, Sera)
  B I Almost Lost My Mind
  C Why Do Fools Fall In Love
  D Singing The Blues   {60% correct on the Internet}

6. On to 1957. This one was by actress Debbie Reynolds, the only female to make it into the top twenty songs for the year. It has been listed as the No. 1 song ever with a girl's name in the title. It came from a movie, and was sung by Debbie to show she was in love.....
  A Diana
  B Donna
  C Glendora
  D Tammy   {80% correct on the Internet}

7. This song has been listed as No. 1 for 1957, and as number fifteen of all-time. It was originally issued as a "B-side". On the charts for over six months it was Pat Boone's biggest hit. It's another sad one, as she made a vow, but broke it and this is the result.....
  A Love Letters In The Sand
  B Moments To Remember
  C All Shook Up
  D Bye Bye Love   {81% correct on the Internet}

8. Let's get back to Elvis. This song has been listed as high as No. 5 for the year, and was number one for seven weeks. It came from a movie of the same name. It was time to boogie, and if you couldn't find a partner, "use a wooden chair".....
  A All Shook Up
  B Jailhouse Rock
  C Whole Lotta Shakin' Goin' On
  D Chain Gang   {95% correct on the Internet}

9. This song was the first hit for Sam Cooke, entering the charts in October, 1957. It was a love song and told all about what this girl did

to Sam. At first, he thought it was just infatuation, but then he decided he wanted to marry her and take her home.....
   A Chances Are
   B You Send Me
   C Wonderful World
   D Wake Up Little Susie   {84% correct on the Internet}

10. The last one from 1957 is essentially an instrumental, although there is some vocalizing, even a few "doo-wahs". Bandleader Jimmy Dorsey performed the song and one source has it on the pop charts for 38 weeks! It's.....
   A Lisbon Antigua
   B Honky Tonk (Parts 1& 2)
   C So Rare
   D Autumn Leaves   {29% correct on the Internet}

11. On to 1958. One source lists this record by Tommy Edwards as No. 1 for the year. Written in 1912 as an instrumental by a future U.S. VP, Charles Dawes, it tells about the up and down world of love.....
   A It's All In The Game
   B My True Love
   C Twilight Time
   D Topsy II   {67% correct on the Internet}

12. This one was the first and biggest hit for The Kingston Trio, and it ranked in the year-end top ten. It's a folk song and the story is that a girl is murdered and the killer is caught by Sheriff Grayson and "this time tomorrow", he'll be "hangin' from a wide oak tree".....
   A Tears On My Pillow
   B Who's Sorry Now
   C Tom Dooley
   D Mr. Lee   {90% correct on the Internet}

13. One big hit for the Big Bopper (J.P. Richardson), killed in the plane crash on "the day the music died", February 3, 1959. It's about that cutie who's got a pretty face and "a pony-tail, hangin' down", plus more, all of which "makes the world go 'round".....
   A Great Balls Of Fire
   B Little Star

   C Rockin' Robin
   D Chantilly Lace   {94% correct on the Internet}

14. Listed in one source as the No. 2 song of 1958, it was one of the biggest hits for the Everly Brothers. This ballad was about unrequited love, "I can make you mine, taste your lips of wine, anytime, night or day".....
   A Lonesome Town
   B Poor Little Fool
   C Dreamin'
   D All I Have To Do Is Dream   {88% correct on the Internet}

15. On to 1959. Since it was the No. 1 song of the year and it was by Bobby Darin, you may already know the answer. It was originally written as the main theme for the "Threepenny Opera" and may well be the most-played "oldie" of all-time.....
   A Dream Lover
   B You Light Up My Life
   C Whoomp! (There It Is)
   D Mack The Knife   {76% correct on the Internet}

16. Another huge hit from 1959, this one was done by Frankie Avalon. It was Frankie's biggest hit and helped turn him into a movie star. Addressed to an entity not normally sung to, surely these things he asks "can't be too great a task".....
   A Mr. Blue
   B Battle Hymn Of The Republic
   C Venus
   D A Boy Named Sue   {90% correct on the Internet}

17. Time for a song from 1959, by Wilbert Harrison. Wilbert is going somewhere and will be standing on the corner of Twelfth Street and Vine. "They got some crazy little women there" and he's gonna' get him one.....
   A Kansas City
   B El Paso
   C Tallahassee Lassie
   D Way Down Yonder In New Orleans {80% correct on the Internet}

18. A very nice song next, a big hit for the Browns, a brother and two sisters. Ranked as high as No. 6 for the year, the song tells the short version of the life of Jimmy Brown (no relation). It begins, "There's a village, hidden deep in the valley".....
   A Quiet Village
   B The Three Bells
   C Among My Souvenirs
   D Lonely Street   {52% correct on the Internet}

19. The No. 2 song for the year was by Johnny Horton, once known as "The Singing Fisherman". It was an historical song and based on a 19th century fiddle tune. We hear about Ol' Hickory, and using 'gators to shoot cannonballs.....
   A Sink The Bismarck
   B Waterloo
   C Philadelphia Freedom
   D The Battle Of New Orleans   {82% correct on the Internet}

20. The last song of this game was by The Coasters and was all about a juvenile delinquent, of a sort. He called the English teacher "dadd-i-o", may have started a fire in the auditorium and played craps in the gym. He said, "Why's everybody always pickin' on me".....
   A Stagger Lee
   B Big, Bad John
   C Johnny Angel
   D Charlie Brown   {89% correct on the Internet}

GAME 3 - WHO SANG THESE? (50s/60s)

Some of these are easy, and some are pretty tough.....we're going way back in time. You need to match the songs to the artists. Top ten tunes are in caps.

1. MOMENTS TO REMEMBER; NO, NOT MUCH!; STANDING ON THE CORNER; WHO NEEDS YOU; PUT A LIGHT IN THE WINDOW.....
   A The Three Degrees
   B The G-Clefs
   C The Four Lads
   D The Four Coins   {62% correct on the Internet}

2. YAKETY YAK; CHARLIE BROWN; ALONG CAME JONES; POISON IVY; SEARCHIN'.....
   A The Coasters
   B Dick And Deedee
   C The Chipmunks
   D The Diamonds   {92% correct on the Internet}

3. TWILIGHT TIME; MY PRAYER; THE GREAT PRETENDER; SMOKE GETS IN YOUR EYES; ONLY YOU (AND YOU ALONE).....
   A The Platters
   B The Cookies
   C Dicky Doo And The Don'ts
   D The Flamingos   {96% correct on the Internet}

4. BYE BYE LOVE; WAKE UP LITTLE SUSIE; ALL I HAVE TO DO IS DREAM; BIRD DOG; PROBLEMS.....
   A The Silhouettes
   B Billy And Lilly
   C The Dell-Vikings
   D The Everly Brothers   {96% correct on the Internet}

5. THAT'LL BE THE DAY; PEGGY SUE; OH, BOY!; Maybe Baby; It Doesn't Matter Anymore.....
   A The Crew-Cuts
   B Buddy Holly/The Crickets
   C The Champs
   D The Royal Teens   {100% correct on the Internet}

6. (WE'RE GONNA) ROCK AROUND THE CLOCK; BURN THAT CANDLE; SEE YOU LATER ALLIGATOR; R-O-C-K.....
   A Johnny Maddox And The Rhythmasters
   B The Oneders
   C Bill Haley And His Comets
   D Flash Cadillac & The Continental Kids   {98% correct on the Internet}

7. ("Obscure group" question.....get ready).....BORN TO BE WITH YOU; LOLLIPOP; JUST BETWEEN YOU AND ME.....
   A The Flirtations
   B A Flock Of Pigeons
   C The Chordettes
   D Kathy Young And The Innocents   {71% correct on the Internet}

8. I ALMOST LOST MY MIND; LOVE LETTERS IN THE SAND; APRIL LOVE; A WONDERFUL TIME UP THERE; REMEMBER YOU'RE MINE.....
   A Ritchie Valens
   B Tommy Edwards
   C Sheb Wooley
   D Pat Boone   {85% correct on the Internet}

9. POOR LITTLE FOOL; LONESOME TOWN; NEVER BE ANYONE ELSE BUT YOU; IT'S LATE; SWEETER THAN YOU.....
   A Sam Cooke
   B Ozzie Nelson
   C Perry Como
   D Ricky Nelson   {80% correct on the Internet}

10. (LET ME BE YOUR) TEDDY BEAR; DON'T; HARD HEADED WOMAN; TOO MUCH; I WANT YOU, I NEED YOU, I LOVE YOU.....
   A Allen Freed
   B Johnny Ray
   C Nervous Norvus
   D Elvis Presley   {90% correct on the Internet}

11. HONEYCOMB; KISSES SWEETER THAN WINE; OH-OH, I'M FALLING IN LOVE AGAIN; SECRETLY; ARE YOU REALLY MINE.....
   A Andy Williams
   B Jimmie Rodgers
   C The Big Bopper
   D Wallace Cleaver   {64% correct on the Internet}

12. MAYBELLENE; SCHOOL DAY; ROCK & ROLL MUSIC; SWEET LITTLE SIXTEEN; JOHNNY B. GOODE.....
   A Chuck Berry
   B Duane Eddy
   C Dave "Baby" Cortez
   D Eddie Cochran   {98% correct on the Internet}

13. BLUE MONDAY; I'M WALKIN'; WHOLE LOTTA LOVING; AIN'T IT A SHAME; BLUEBERRY HILL.....
   A Buddy Knox
   B Chubby Checker
   C Tubby Thompson
   D Fats Domino   {88% correct on the Internet}

14. IT'S NOT FOR ME TO SAY; CHANCES ARE; THE TWELFTH OF NEVER; Wonderful, Wonderful; Misty.....
   A Harry Belafonte
   B Johnny Mathis
   C Kenny Dexter
   D Sal Mineo   {91% correct on the Internet}

15. SPLISH SPLASH; QUEEN OF THE HOP; DREAM LOVER; MACK THE KNIFE.....
   A Fabian
   B Jerry Lee Lewis
   C Bobby Darin
   D Jackie Wilson   {88% correct on the Internet}

16. VENUS; DEDE DINAH; BOBBY SOX TO STOCKINGS; JUST ASK YOUR HEART; WHY.....
   A Perez Prado
   B Tab Hunter
   C Ed Norton
   D Frankie Avalon   {96% correct on the Internet}

17. WHO'S SORRY NOW; LIPSTICK ON YOUR COLLAR; FRANKIE; MY HAPPINESS; AMONG MY SOUVENIRS.....
   A Laurie London
   B April Paris
   C Connie Francis
   D Annette   {92% correct on the Internet}

18. LONG TALL SALLY; GOOD GOLLY, MISS MOLLY; KEEP A KNOCKIN'; JENNY, JENNY; Tutti-Frutti.....
   A Little Richard
   B Little Anthony
   C Tommy Edwards
   D Tony Orlando   {99% correct on the Internet}

19. DIANA; YOU ARE MY DESTINY; LONELY BOY; PUT YOUR HEAD ON MY SHOULDER; IT'S TIME TO CRY.....
   A Paul Anka
   B Andy Williams
   C Harry Chiti
   D Freddy Cannon   {95% correct on the Internet}

20. ("Extra-tough" solo singer question.....get ready)......IVORY TOWER; DARK MOON; I HEAR YOU KNOCKING; MEMORIES ARE MADE OF THIS; TEEN AGE PRAYER.....
   A Barbara Springer
   B Annie Oakley
   C Gale Storm
   D Gogi Grant   {45% correct on the Internet}

GAME 4 - SUBTITLES FROM THE 50s/60s

This game is all about subtitles. After reading the clues, you need to select the correct subtitle for the song in question.

1. We will start with a 1962 hit from Bobby Vinton, who had quite a few hits in the early 60s. This one was called ROSES ARE RED and it launched Bobby's singing career. Be careful on this subtitle.....
   A (Violets Are Blue)
   B (Just For You)
   C (Daffodils Are Yellow)
   D (My Love)   {43% correct on the Internet}

2. One of Neil Diamond's biggest hits (one of his three platinum records) was SWEET CAROLINE from 1969. The subtitle gives a summary of what the song is all about.....
   A (You'll Be A Woman Soon)
   B (Good Times Never Seemed So Good)
   C (How's Everything Going?)
   D (Love Every Time I Turn Around)   {91% correct on the Internet}

3. In 1958, The Four Preps had their biggest hit with a gold record called 26 MILES (not to be confused with Edwin Starr's Twenty-Five Miles). It stayed at No. 2 for three weeks. The subtitle.....
   A (About 42 Kilometers)
   B (Across The Sea)
   C (Santa Catalina)
   D (Almost A Marathon)   {44% correct on the Internet}

4. In 1964, The Four Seasons had a pretty memorable hit with a song called DAWN. Hopefully, you remember what they told Dawn to do.....
   A (Let's Hang On)
   B (Shake Your Groove Thing)
   C (Be Mine)
   D (Go Away)   {65% correct on the Internet}

5. In a song which became one of the anthems of the peace movement of the late 60s, Buffalo Springfield made it to No. 7 in 1967 with FOR WHAT IT'S WORTH. The subtitle might be even more memorable.....
  A (Stop, Hey What's That Sound)
  B (We're On The Eve Of Destruction)
  C (Paranoia Strikes Deep)
  D (War Is Hell)   {76% correct on the Internet}

6. While we're at it, let's go with another 1967 song which became an anthem for the hippie/peace movement. It was by Scott McKenzie and was called SAN FRANCISCO. The subtitle gave instructions.....
  A (Go West, Young Man)
  B (Take The A Train)
  C (Be Sure To Wear Flowers In Your Hair)
  D (Give Peace A Chance)   {87% correct on the Internet}

7. Now we're going all the way back to 1956, for the year's No. 6 hit. It was by Doris Day and called WHATEVER WILL BE, WILL BE. The song won an Oscar as the best song from a movie for that year. The subtitle.....
  A (Is That All There Is?)
  B (La Cocina)
  C (Que Sera, Sera)
  D (C'est La Vie)   {97% correct on the Internet}

8. Since we are back in the 50s, we'll stay here for a bit. In 1957, Marty Robbins had his only pop gold record with A WHITE SPORT COAT. The subtitle told of something else that night.....
  A (And A Pink Carnation)
  B (And Black Slacks)
  C (And Tan Shoe And Pink Shoelaces)
  D (And Empty Arms)   {86% correct on the Internet}

9. In the same year, Harry Belafonte also had a gold record with a song called BANANA BOAT. This song had a very memorable refrain, which is the subtitle.....
  A (Right On)
  B (Work All Day)

C (Day-O)
   D (Carry Me Bananas)   {90% correct on the Internet}

10. Back to the 60s, we will do one which shouldn't be too tough, from 1964. It was by Jan and Dean and was all about THE LITTLE OLD LADY. This is one that just needs that subtitle.....
   A (Her Name Is Gina)
   B (From Mendecino)
   C (In The Casino)
   D (From Pasadena)   {98% correct on the Internet}

11. The next song was from 1968 and by John Fred and His Playboy Band. It was the No.9 song of that year, called JUDY IN DISGUISE. It was supposedly a parody of the Beatles' Lucy In The Sky With Diamonds. The subtitle was.....
   A (That's What You Are)
   B (With Glasses)
   C (Canteloupe Eyes)
   D (With Rubies)   {67% correct on the Internet}

12. One of the biggest hits of 1958 was HE'S GOT THE WHOLE WORLD, recorded by the one-hit wonder Laurie London. Laurie was a male, recording the song at age thirteen. The subtitle.....
   A (On His Shoulders)
   B (In His Hands)
   C (In His Sight)
   D (To Worry About)   {98% correct on the Internet}

13. How about a nice soul song from 1969 and Jr. Walker & The All Stars. It was called WHAT DOES IT TAKE and made it to No. 4. The subtitle.....
   A (To Get You Next To Me)
   B (Anyway)
   C (To Show I'm Not A Fake)
   D (To Win Your Love)   {69% correct on the Internet}

14. Another tune from 1969 from another one-hit wonder was LOVE, by Mercy. Of course, it's one of many that begins with the word love, but one of the few with a subtitle.....

A (Can Make You Happy)
B (Nip It In The Bud)
C (Is All We Need)
D (Is All Around) {61% correct on the Internet}

15. In 1966, a studio group called The T-Bones made it to No. 3 with an instrumental called NO MATTER WHAT SHAPE. The tune was used as a jingle for Alka-Seltzer. The subtitle.....
A (Your Stomach's In)
B (Get It Together)
C (Work It Out)
D (Plop, Plop, Fizz, Fizz) {48% correct on the Internet}

16. In 1967, Engelbert Humperdinck (born Arnold George Dorsey) had one of his biggest pop hits with RELEASE ME. This song had been a country hit in 1954. The subtitle.....
A (From The Prison Of Your Heart)
B (It's Sayonara Time)
C (And Let Me Love Again)
D (It's All Over, Anyway) {91% correct on the Internet}

17. A group called the Crystals made it to No. 3 in 1963, with a song called DA DOO RON RON. If you remember the song, you may remember that the subtitle came before the title in the song.....
A (And Then He Kissed Me)
B (Is All I Want To Say To You)
C (I Met Him At The Candy Store)
D (When He Walked Me Home) {59% correct on the Internet}

18. Keeping with the "silly" titles, in 1964, Betty Everett had a No. 6 hit with a song called THE SHOOP SHOOP SONG. The subtitle was to help you know if "he loves you so".....
A (Oogum Boogum Song)
B (It's In His Kiss)
C (That's Just The Way It Is, Baby)
D (It Only Takes A Minute) {94% correct on the Internet}

19. Sorry, but we can't resist including this unforgettable (?) 1961 number from Lonnie Donegan And His Skiffle Group (it did make it to No. 5). It was called DOES YOUR CHEWING GUM LOSE ITS FLAVOR.....
   A (After Chewing It For Spite)
   B (When You Use It To Get A Dime From The Sewer)
   C (Somewhere, Over The Rainbow)
   D (On The Bedpost Overnight)   {94% correct on the Internet}

20. You may well remember the song IN THE YEAR 2525 by Zager & Evans. It was No. 1 for six weeks in 1969! But, do you know the odd subtitle.....
   A (Skeleton Army)
   B (Gammon The Twelve)
   C (Exordium & Terminus)
   D (You Want A Little Memory Powder)   {69% correct on the Internet}

GAME 5 - SAILIN' THROUGH THE 60s

You may want to listen to your collection of 60s hits before tackling this game.

1. This song by the Kingsmen has probably the most misunderstood lyrics of any song. If you ever see the real lyrics, you'll realize that they really don't tell us what happens every night, at ten.....
   A Blame It On The Bossa Nova
   B Come A Little Bit Closer
   C Playboy
   D Louie, Louie   {89% correct on the Internet}

2. The guy in this song wasn't very well-liked. He was a non-conformist from the word go. But the Crystals were proud of him. Still, they said he'd never be any good, because.....
   A He's So Shy
   B He Don't Love You (Like I Love You)
   C He's A Rebel
   D (He's The) Leader Of The Pack   {63% correct on the Internet}

3. And then there's the Chiffons. They like this guy who's got wavy hair and is the envy of all the girls. If the singer was a queen, she'd even leave her throne for him. This is what they say about him:
   A He's Got The Whole World (In His Hands)
   B He's So Shy
   C He's So Fine
   D He Ain't Heavy, He's My Brother   {97% correct on the Internet}

4. Neil Sedaka is upset. He's having a problem with his honey and he simply wants to "start anew". Not only that, but he really wishes that they were making up again. He is claiming.....
   A Breaking Up Is Hard To Do
   B I'm "The One Who Really Loves You"
   C Big Girls Don't Cry
   D I'm "Running Scared"   {93% correct on the Internet}

5. The Toys are so happy. And we are happy for them. It's 1965 and they are in the meadow, the birds are serenading away, and everything is wonderful. So, they sing.....
   A Lover's Concerto
   B I Got You Babe
   C The Mountain Of Love
   D The Birds And The Bees   {34% correct on the Internet}

6. Things can be so tough in the world of rock and roll. Now, Gary Lewis and the Playboys want to give something away, due to a broken heart. They will give this to you, if you have a lover who's faithful.....
   A Ticket To Ride
   B Mockingbird
   C Love Potion #9
   D This Diamond Ring   {83% correct on the Internet}

7. So, the Beach Boys have lost a girl. She was apparently perfect, but this situation may have a happy ending, if their plea is answered:
   A Go Away Little Girl
   B I Want You Back
   C Hit the Road Jack
   D Help Me, Rhonda   {93% correct on the Internet}

8. We'll get to some happier songs eventually, but now the Righteous Brothers will have tears on their pillows. There won't be any happy ending here -- something beautiful is dying, because.....
   A She's Not There
   B You've Lost That Loving Feeling
   C These Boots Were Made For Walking
   D England Swings   {97% correct on the Internet}

9. Sam the Sham & the Pharoahs had the Billboard Record of the Year in 1965. The words are almost as difficult to understand as the Kingsmen's (see above). The name came from Sam's cat.....
   A Wooly Bully
   B Hanky Panky
   C Sukiyaki
   D Hang On Sloopy   {93% correct on the Internet}

10. Sonny and Cher -- they were young and in love in 1965. Anyway, Sonny's hair may have been too long, but there was no hill or mountain they couldn't climb, because.....
   A I'll Never Find Another You
   B Apple, Peaches, Pumpkin Pie
   C I Got You Babe
   D Everybody Loves A Clown   {98% correct on the Internet}

11. The Ad Libs describe this fine young man. He's no clown, lives in a penthouse and even wears a mohair suit. You oughta come and see the.....
   A Soul Man
   B Boy From New York City
   C Mr. Tambourine Man
   D Cool Jerk   {75% correct on the Internet}

12. Randy and the Rainbows, dooby doo; they are in love, dooby doo; they have a crush on her, dooby doo; when they walk, dooby doo; it seems like paradise, dooby doo. She is.....
   A Dominique
   B Rag Doll
   C Denise
   D Mother-in-Law   {61% correct on the Internet}

13. This was from the musical Hair. Oliver sings of...early morning singin' song, lovin' and laughin' a song, and dooby abba dobba (or something like that); it's.....
   A Good Morning Starshine
   B Bad Moon Rising
   C Crystal Blue Persuasion
   D Jumpin' Jack Flash   {92% correct on the Internet}

14. This one by the Nashville Teens could be depressing, if it weren't so upbeat. After all, momma died and daddy got drunk, in a rusty shack. Do you know the name of the place they loathe?
   A A World Without Love
   B In The Ghetto
   C Tobacco Road
   D Winchester Cathedral   {76% correct on the Internet}

15. The Classics IV, with Dennis Yost, sang of torn tickets, faded photographs, hair ribbons, rings once worn, and love letters, which were, sadly.....
   A Sounds Of Silence
   B Crystal Blue Persuasion
   C The Good, The Bad And The Ugly
   D Traces   {82% correct on the Internet}

16. There are fellas hanging around her all the time (she must have been the cat's pajamas). We don't find out what her name is, but she sure did affect Tommy Roe. She makes him.....
   A Dizzy
   B (A) Daydream Believer
   C Mr. Tambourine Man
   D Gitarzan   {93% correct on the Internet}

17. We just can't get away from the tearjerkers, can we? Del Shannon just had his girl leave him and he's in pain. He's spending the night walking in the rain, looking for her and wondering where she's gone. She's his little.....
   A Runaround Sue
   B Wanderer
   C Runaway
   D Wild One   {88% correct on the Internet}

18. This song has been ranked in the top 200 of the all-time top rock 'n' roll songs. Ben E. King has a request and he's not asking for much; he won't be afraid if his darling will just.....
   A Stand By Me
   B Please, Please Me
   C Play That Funky Music
   D Please Come To Boston   {98% correct on the Internet}

19. Around the same time that Chubby Checker was a twisting fool, he was also promoting this dance. He wanted a big, boss line, in the Union Hall. Boogety, boogety, shoo, it's.....
  A The Hokey Pokey
  B Tie Me Kangaroo Down, Sport
  C Pony Time
  D Monkey Time   {57% correct on the Internet}

20. The Drifters needed a place to go after a hard day's work. The place had fresh (and sweet) air, and at night you would get a free star show. It's.....
  A Spanish Harlem
  B Blueberry Hill
  C Winchester Cathedral
  D Up On The Roof   {82% correct on the Internet}

GAME 6 - SARCASTIC 60s

These are all pretty popular songs from the 60s....and we've managed to tear them down, just a little bit.....they don't get no respect!

1. "SUGAR SHACK" BY JIMMY GILMER AND THE FIREBALLS --all you have to do is recall what the shack was made of:
   A bricks
   B wood
   C straw
   D dreams
   E sugar   {45% correct on the Internet}

2. "SURF CITY" BY JAN & DEAN -- Okay, if you go to Surf City, there are "two swingin' honeys for every guy" - (we can presume that appearance doesn't matter); to get your pair, all you need to do is:
   A take a ride
   B just say hi
   C buy them fries
   D wink your eye
   E smile and sigh   {64% correct on the Internet}

3. "IT'S MY PARTY" BY LESLEY GORE -- Poor Lesley! She loses her boyfriend to that conniving, deceitful other girl! At her birthday party, no less! (It must be Lesley's turn to cry.) Who are the two that break her heart?
   A Johnny and Judy
   B Billy and Bobby
   C Ralph and Alice
   D Eddie and Marcie
   E Danny and Donna   {90% correct on the Internet}

4. "IF YOU WANNA BE HAPPY" BY JIMMY SOUL -- Some rude person tells the singer that he saw his wife the other day and that she is quite repulsive-looking. The singer actually agrees with this, but says he's happy because she sure can _____, baby!

A clean
   B dance
   C kiss
   D cook
   E love me   {49% correct on the Internet}

5. "EASIER SAID THAN DONE" BY THE ESSEX -- Boy, some people know everything! In this song, the singer's friends are filled with advice for the lovelorn. Which of the following is NOT given as a solution to her problem:
   A sing to him
   B just do anything for him
   C swing with him
   D tell him "he's the one"
   E have a fling with him   {67% correct on the Internet}

6. "MY BOYFRIEND'S BACK" BY THE ANGELS -- All right, so he's back. Big deal! (No doubt, she enjoyed the attention while her main squeeze was off who-knows-where.) Anyway, now she tells the guy who's been chasing her to take a:
   A long walk on a short pier
   B permanent vacation
   C trip to the moon
   D little tip from me
   E fast train outta town   {77% correct on the Internet}

7. "BREAD AND BUTTER" BY THE NEWBEATS -- So what is this song all about? Is there some hidden meaning here, or not? The singer comes home early one day and finds his baby and some other guy eating:
   A chicken and dumplings
   B spaghetti and meatballs
   C crackers and cheese
   D milk and honey
   E curds and whey   {29% correct on the Internet}

8. "UNDER THE BOARDWALK" BY THE DRIFTERS -- If you get tired of this, you can always go up on the roof. But while you're down there with all the spiders, you can hear the happy sounds of what, from a nearby park?
  A a roller coaster
  B a carousel
  C a wishing well
  D children
  E thirty-seven high school students on a field trip   {75% correct on the Internet}

9. "I GET AROUND" BY THE BEACH BOYS -- Life is great. You're on top of the world and free to do just about anything you want. Even the _____ left the Beach Boys alone:
  A police
  B bad guys
  C girlfriends
  D old folks
  E record company technicians   {62% correct on the Internet}

10. "THE LITTLE OLD LADY (FROM PASADENA)" BY JAN & DEAN -- So, granny drives this super stock red Dodge and acquires a reputation of sorts along the way. She is, or was (she's probably in racecar heaven, after all):
  A an L.A. granny with rubber to burn
  B the nightmare of pedestrians everywhere
  C the scourge of California Ocean Drive
  D cruisin' to the hamburger stand
  E the terror of Colorado Boulevard   {61% correct on the Internet}

11. _____BY THE DIXIE CUPS -- We'll try a little something different here. One, some, or all of the Dixie Cups are going to get married. (This time they're really sure.) Where are they going, in order to tie the knot?
  A The Little Brown Church in the Dale
  B My Home Town
  C The Chapel of Love
  D Las Vegas
  E The Village of Love   {95% correct on the Internet}

12. "LAST KISS" BY J. FRANK WILSON AND THE CAVALIERS -- C'mon, J. Frank, YOU crashed the car. Take some of the blame yourself, for Pete's sake. Anyway, her last words were apparently:
   A Give me a little kiss, will ya, huh?
   B Tell me that you love me.
   C Hold me, darlin', for a little while.
   D Don't forget me, my dear.
   E Frankly, my dear, I don't give a damn.   {65% correct on the Internet}

13. "LEADER OF THE PACK" BY THE SHANGRI-LAS -- Poor Jimmy probably never would have contributed much to the global economy, but his death was senseless anyway. Where did he and Betty meet?
   A the laundromat
   B the beach
   C school
   D the dance
   E the candy store   {76% correct on the Internet}

14. "THE NAME GAME" BY SHIRLEY ELLIS -- Remember when we all played this game for hours on end? Which of the following names was not used in the song? (The correct answer works, though. Try it.)
   A Shirley
   B Georgie
   C Lincoln
   D Marsha
   E Nick   {45% correct on the Internet}

15. "EVE OF DESTRUCTION" BY BARRY MCGUIRE -- Pretty depressing song, huh? After telling us to think of all the hate there is in Red China (does that make sense?), we then have to "look around" to _____, to find hate in our "own backyard". Ouch!
   A Los Angeles, California
   B Selma, Alabama
   C Jackson, Mississippi
   D New York City, NY
   E Mayberry, NC   {58% correct on the Internet}

16. "I'M A BELIEVER" BY THE MONKEES -- Not much to this song. Most of the Monkees' songs were okay...good enough to enjoy once every couple of years. Anyway, what actually made "believers" out of the not-so-fab-four?
    A then I saw her face
    B then she called my name
    C then she walked her walk
    D then she blew in my ear
    E then she kissed my lips   {95% correct on the Internet}

17. "SUMMER IN THE CITY" BY THE LOVIN' SPOONFUL -- Remember the jackhammers? And what happens to the back of his neck, anyway? Now, if he finds a "kitty", he is going to meet her, apparently at night, where?
    A on the rooftop
    B under the boardwalk
    C at the beach
    D at the bus stop
    E at the candy store   {64% correct on the Internet}

18. "WILD THING" BY THE TROGGS -- So, are good lyrics really all that important? But the "wild thing" must have been really something! After all, she...
    A was his everything
    B made him feel like a king
    C made his bell ring
    D made his heart sing
    E made his blood boil   {94% correct on the Internet}

19. "HANKY PANKY" BY TOMMY JAMES AND THE SHONDELLS -- Have you actually ever seen anyone doing the hanky panky? Maybe on American Bandstand. Anyway, where did he actually see his baby for the very first time?
    A walkin' with the sand beneath her feet
    B on the dance floor, doing the HP
    C at the scene, now, where they're doin' that thing
    D at school, lookin' so fine
    E walkin' on down the line   {53% correct on the Internet}

20. "MONDAY, MONDAY" BY THE MAMAS & THE PAPAS --
So, what's the story here? Did someone's lover leave on Monday? Why are the other days of the week fine? In any case, whenever Monday comes around, you'll find this person "_____ all of the time."
  A working
  B crying
  C hiding
  D dreaming
  E remembering   {75% correct on the Internet}

GAME 7 - MORE SARCASTIC 60s

These are mostly from the early 60s, and we don't want you to take these too seriously...

1. "WHEN A MAN LOVES A WOMAN" BY PERCY SLEDGE -- Go, Percy! This is quite a problem indeed! According to Percy, all of the following might happen to a man in such condition, except:
   A sleep out in the rain
   B spend his very last dime
   C turn his back on his best friend
   D swim the deepest ocean   {79% correct on the Internet}

2. "DEVIL WITH A BLUE DRESS ON" BY MITCH RYDER & THE DETROIT WHEELS -- This Devil may be wilder than the Wild Thing....high-heel sneakers and an alligator hat!? But, that's too easy. The question is, what kind of perfume does this Devil wear?
   A Gardenia Blossom
   B Chanel No. 5
   C Chantilly
   D Scent of a Woman   {62% correct on the Internet}

3. "GOOD LOVIN' " BY THE YOUNG RASCALS -- This is where the doctor says "Yeah, yeah, yeah, yeah, yeah; yeah, yeah, yeah, yeah, yeah." So the singer tells his baby that it's definite, he's got the _____ and she's got the _____.
   A sickness, potion
   B love jones, answer
   C fever, cure
   D fire, fuel
   E brains, money   {91% correct on the Internet}

4. In 1965, Wayne Fontana and the Mindbenders, from Manchester, England, had the first of their two big hits with GAME OF LOVE. According to this song, the game of love started in the Garden of Eden, when Adam said to Eve.....?
   A "baby, you're for me"
   B "let's get it on"

  C "honey, ignore that tree"
  D "sweetie, love me do"   {62% correct on the Internet}

5. "DUKE OF EARL" BY GENE CHANDLER -- C'mon, Gene, who are you kidding? You're the Duke of Earl? Maybe he used it as a pick-up line, like "Hey, baby, what's your name? I'm the Duke of Earl." Maybe it worked! Anyway, he tells his girl that she'll be:
  A his Queen forevermore
  B the Duchess of Earl
  C the Princess
  D happy in Earl   {60% correct on the Internet}

6. "SOLDIER BOY" BY THE SHIRELLES -- Mr. Soldier Boy gets to take the singer's love to "any port or foreign shore," and she swears to be true. Wonder if he thought of her when he was on R&R? She says that, wherever he goes:
  A my heart will follow
  B I will be waiting
  C you will be electronically monitored
  D my prayers will be with you   {74% correct on the Internet}

7. "SHEILA" BY TOMMY ROE -- Well, isn't this a happy song? Sheila's no devil, nor a wild thing, just a nice sweet girl. The two of them are so happy. And just her name drives him insane! Which best describes cute little Sheila?
  A tall and tan and young and lovely
  B pink curls and a sexy smile
  C blue eyes and a ponytail
  D tan shoes and pink shoelaces   {87% correct on the Internet}

8. "PEPPERMINT TWIST" BY JOEY DEE & THE STARLIGHTERS -- Anyone who tries to do the twist to this song better be in shape. This is no slow twistin'. The question is, where do the Peppermint Twisters meet?
  A at the bowling alley
  B Hollywood and Vine
  C down on 45th Street
  D up on the roof
  E at choir practice   {55% correct on the Internet}

9. "THE LOCO-MOTION" BY LITTLE EVA -- To do this dance, you need at least two things -- just a little rhythm, but a lot of soul. Oh, look! They're making a chain! This dance is so simple, even who can do it with ease?
   A her mother and her father
   B her little baby sister
   C her boppin' little grandma
   D the neighbors down the street
   E the loco loco-motorman   {79% correct on the Internet}

10. "THE WANDERER" BY DION -- He sure is something; he must be one of the top five "Mr. Machos" of the rock-n-roll era. If this were the 90s, Madonna would be chasing him. Name the lucky girl who'll be with him tonight.
    A Blondie
    B Janie
    C Shontel
    D Rebecca
    E Madonna   {84% correct on the Internet}

11. "JOHNNY ANGEL" BY SHELLEY FABARES -- Shelley says that this Mr. Wonderful doesn't even know that she exists, but he has said "hello" to her more than once. In fact, what happens everytime he says "hello".
    A she gets all tongue-tied
    B her heart begins to fly
    C she whispers "my, oh, my"
    D she sits right down and cries
    E she'd like a piece of pie   {70% correct on the Internet}

12. "PALISADES PARK" BY FREDDY CANNON -- Freddy sure had a great time on this outing. He meets a girl, they eat a lot at a hot dog stand, and they hug in the Tunnel of Love. He also gets a great kiss, where?
    A on the chute-de-chutes
    B right on the lips
    C at the top of the ferris wheel
    D under the boardwalk   {71% correct on the Internet}

13. "LAND OF 1000 DANCES" BY CANNIBAL AND THE HEADHUNTERS -- You can probably even do the Hucklebuck there. Let's go to the first dance mentioned....you have to know how to pony, like....
   A Bony Marone
   B Billy and Tony
   C A phony baloney
   D you're all on your own-y   {84% correct on the Internet}

14. "C'MON AND SWIM" BY BOBBY FREEMAN -- No doubt you can do this one in the land of 1000 dances. Which of these other dances is NOT mentioned in this song? (hint: this is from the 60s.)
   A the Monkey
   B the Twist
   C the Stroll
   D the Hully Gully   {38% correct on the Internet}

15. "THE TWIST" BY CHUBBY CHECKER -- Just like Little Eva and the Locomotion, Chubby's got a relative that can do his dance very well. So, if you want to see the dance, you should see....
   A my cousin Chris
   B my little sis
   C my Aunt Alice
   D my Mama Tish   {84% correct on the Internet}

16. "STAGGER LEE" BY LLOYD PRICE -- This song tells a story. There's gambling going on, and Stagger gets angry and goes home for his .44. He takes it back to the barroom and....
   A holds up the place
   B shoots himself
   C shoots Billy
   D shoots everyone
   E starts a gun-control petition   {79% correct on the Internet}

17. "MOCKINGBIRD" BY CHARLES AND INEZ FOXX -- Mock, yeah......ing, yeah.....bird, yeah.....yeah, yeah; so, he's going to buy her a mockingbird and if that bird doesn't sing, he'll buy her....
   A a backyard swing
   B my ding-a-ling
   C a diamond ring
   D a bell to ring
   E some other thing   {97% correct on the Internet}

18. "RAINDROPS" BY DEE CLARK -- This song was conceived while Dee was driving from New York to Chicago in a rainstorm. After his love left him, he's all alone; he would bring her back, but....
   A she was leaving on a jet plane
   B she ran off with another
   C she said, "Get lost, Chump!"
   D he doesn't know where she's gone
   E he wasn't paying attention and drove off the road   {68% correct on the Internet}

19. "RESCUE ME" BY FONTELLA BASS -- Fontella's obviously got a love jones. Could she be chasing the Duke of Earl? The Wanderer? What matches those would be! So, what, actually, does Fontella ask to be rescued from?
   A loneliness and "blueness"
   B the arms of another
   C the daily rat race
   D a crazed stalker
   E bad lyrics   {74% correct on the Internet}

20. "MOTHER-IN-LAW" BY ERNIE K. DOE -- Another sad lament. It has to be one of the only songs with a reference to the Constitution. Which of the following phrases is NOT used to describe the "lovely lady"?
   A Satan should be her name
   B as bad as she can be
   C the worst person I know
   D sent from down below   {30% correct on the Internet}

GAME 8 - WHO SANG THESE? (60s)

Just match the artist with the hits.....if it's in caps, the song made the top ten.

1. IT'S ALL RIGHT; KEEP ON PUSHING; AMEN; Gypsy Woman; People Get Ready; Talking About My Baby.....
   A Delfonics
   B Impressions
   C Reparata and the Delrons
   D Spinners   {49% correct on the Internet}

2. WALK LIKE A MAN; RAG DOLL; LET'S HANG ON; Stay; Big Man In Town; Bye, Bye, Baby (Baby Goodbye).....
   A Four Seasons
   B Four Lads
   C Four Tops
   D Four Flushers   {91% correct on the Internet}

3. A GIRL LIKE YOU; PEOPLE GOT TO BE FREE; A BEAUTIFUL MORNING; I've Been Lonely Too Long; You Better Run; It's Wonderful.....
   A Vogues
   B Rivingtons
   C Beach Boys
   D (Young) Rascals   {85% correct on the Internet}

4. CRIMSON AND CLOVER; SWEET CHERRY WINE; I THINK WE'RE ALONE NOW; MIRAGE; MONY,MONY; CRYSTAL BLUE PERSUASION.....
   A Gary Lewis & The Playboys
   B Association
   C Tommy James & The Shondells
   D Animals   {87% correct on the Internet}

5. DON'T MESS WITH BILL; PLEASE MR. POSTMAN; PLAYBOY; Beechwood 4-5789; The Hunter Gets Captured By The Game; My Baby Must Be A Magician.....

   A Shangri-Las
   B Shirelles
   C Rochell & The Candles
   D Marvelettes   {45% correct on the Internet}

6. I'VE GOTTA GET A MESSAGE TO YOU; I STARTED A JOKE; To Love Somebody; Massachusetts; Words; New York Mining Disaster 1941.....
   A Box Tops
   B Gary Puckett & The Union Gap
   C Classics IV
   D Bee Gees   {74% correct on the Internet}

7. HUNGRY; HIM OR ME - WHAT'S IT GONNA BE?; GOOD THING; Just Like Me; I Had A Dream; Too Much Talk.....
   A Monkees
   B Paul Revere & The Raiders
   C Outsiders
   D Lovin' Spoonful   {62% correct on the Internet}

8. THE LAST TIME; AS TEARS GO BY; MOTHERS LITTLE HELPER; HAVE YOU SEEN YOUR MOTHER, BABY, STANDING IN THE SHADOW; Heart Of Stone; Dandelion.....
   A Rolling Stones
   B Sly & The Family Stone
   C Linda Ronstadt & The Stone Poneys
   D Quarrymen   {80% correct on the Internet}

9. SHE CRIED; COME A LITTLE BIT CLOSER; CARA MIA; THIS MAGIC MOMENT; Some Enchanted Evening; Let's Lock The Door (And Throw Away The Key).....
   A Four Seasons
   B Gerry & The Pacemakers
   C Kinks
   D Jay & The Americans   {61% correct on the Internet}

10. STONED SOUL PICNIC; UP-UP AND AWAY; WEDDING BELL BLUES; Go Where You Wanna Go; Sweet Blindness; Workin' On A Groovy Thing.....
   A Spanky & Our Gang
   B Gladys Knight & The Pips
   C 5th Dimension
   D Supremes   {89% correct on the Internet}

11. (THE MAN WHO SHOT) LIBERTY VALANCE; IT HURTS TO BE IN LOVE; Town Without Pity; Twenty Four Hours From Tulsa; Mecca; She's A Heartbreaker.....
   A John Wayne
   B Bobby Rydell
   C Gene Pitney
   D Johnny Rivers   {62% correct on the Internet}

12. CHAIN GANG; TWISTIN' THE NIGHT AWAY; ANOTHER SATURDAY NIGHT; Bring It On Home To Me; Wonderful World; Cupid.....
   A Chubby Checker
   B Sam Cooke
   C Ray Charles
   D Pat Boone   {79% correct on the Internet}

13. HOW SWEET IT IS TO BE LOVED BY YOU; I HEARD IT THROUGH THE GRAPEVINE; AIN'T THAT PECULIAR; I'LL BE DOGGONE; Try It Baby; You're A Wonderful One.....
   A Marvin Gaye
   B Bruce Channel
   C Johnny Mathis
   D Stevie Wonder   {94% correct on the Internet}

14. ROSES ARE RED (MY LOVE); BLUE VELVET; MR. LONELY; THERE! I'VE SAID IT AGAIN; PLEASE LOVE ME FOREVER; BLUE ON BLUE.....
   A Rick Nelson
   B Jackie Wilson
   C Bobby Vee
   D Bobby Vinton   {83% correct on the Internet}

15. SHE'S NOT YOU; BOSSA NOVA BABY; (MARIE'S THE NAME) HIS LATEST FLAME; SURRENDER; If I Can Dream; Puppet On A String.....
   A Elvis Presley
   B Dean Martin
   C Roy Orbison
   D Wilson Pickett   {45% correct on the Internet}

16. SWEET NOTHIN'S; DUM DUM; ALL ALONE AM I; I'M SORRY; Coming On Strong; Rockin' Around The Christmas Tree.....
   A Connie Francis
   B The Singing Nun
   C Brenda Lee
   D Nancy Sinatra   {66% correct on the Internet}

17. WALK ON BY; MESSAGE TO MICHAEL; I SAY A LITTLE PRAYER; DO YOU KNOW THE WAY TO SAN JOSE; Alfie; Promises, Promises.....
   A Mary Wells
   B Barbra Streisand
   C Aretha Franklin
   D Dionne Warwick   {87% correct on the Internet}

18. I KNOW A PLACE; MY LOVE; DON'T SLEEP IN THE SUBWAY; I COULDN'T LIVE WITHOUT YOUR LOVE; A Sign Of The Times; Color My World.....
   A Cher
   B Lulu
   C Lesley Gore
   D Petula Clark   {75% correct on the Internet}

19. SHEILA; EVERYBODY; SWEET PEA; HOORAY FOR HAZEL; DIZZY; JAM UP JELLY TIGHT.....
   A Tommy Roe
   B Nervous Norvus
   C Steve Lawrence
   D Neil Sedaka   {75% correct on the Internet}

20. MELLOW YELLOW; ATLANTIS; SUNSHINE SUPERMAN; HURDY GURDY MAN; Epistle To Dippy; There Is A Mountain.....
   A Bob Dylan
   B Donovan
   C Johnny Rivers
   D Lou Christie   {88% correct on the Internet}

GAME 9 - THE TRICKY 60s

Okay, where did we say that all of these games would be easy? This one sure isn't (after the first question, anyway).

1. "TWIST AND SHOUT" BY THE ISLEY BROTHERS - Yes, also done by the Beatles. In fact, if memory serves, that was the only No. 1 for the Beatles which they didn't compose. So, in this song, what is the only request the singer does NOT make of his partner?
   A shake it up, baby
   B move that thing
   C twist a little closer
   D come on and work it on out   {97% correct on the Internet}

2. "DEDICATED TO THE ONE I LOVE" BY THE SHIRELLES - In this song, there is a fairly simple request. While they are apart, what does the singer ask her lover boy to do, each night before he goes to bed (presumably alone)?
   A write words of love
   B call her on the phone
   C read John 3:10
   D think of their moments together
   E whisper a little prayer for her   {75% correct on the Internet}

3. "JUDY IN DISGUISE" BY JOHN FRED AND HIS PLAYBOY BAND - Yes, this is the girl with the cantaloupe eyes (with glasses). A very strange song, but the late 60s had quite a few of those. Anyway, Judy is told to "cross her heart with".....
   A her green tambourine
   B a new disguise
   C her living bra
   D her gold peace sign
   E anything at all   {55% correct on the Internet}

4. "BROWN EYED GIRL" BY VAN MORRISON - Van and his girl used to slip away quite often, apparently, for a little hanky panky, and they probably weren't dancing. They went to a number of different places, but which one of these did they NOT go to?

   A down to the old mine
   B behind the stadium
   C under Kelsey's bridge
   D down in the hollow   {57% correct on the Internet}

5. "I FOUGHT THE LAW" BY THE BOBBY FULLER FOUR - The law won, but maybe if you play this song enough times, Bobby will actually win once. We can keep hoping, just for a change. So, what did he actually do, which apparently resulted in incarceration?
   A shot the sheriff
   B robbed people with a six-gun
   C held up a mail train
   D went one toke over the line
   E stole the deputy's horse   {77% correct on the Internet}

6. "1-2-3" - BY LEN BARRY - Okay, we will keep this very simple, in line with the theme of the song. It's elementary, my dear player.....falling in love is so easy, it's.....
   A something even the blind can see
   B as easy as pie
   C like taking candy from a baby
   D like doing the Twist
   E like openin' your eyes   {77% correct on the Internet}

7. "AQUARIUS/LET THE SUNSHINE IN" BY THE 5TH DIMENSION - Yes, it's the late 60s and everything is beautiful and mystical and maybe even psychedelic. And, it's the dawning of the Age of Aquarius! According to the song, where is the Moon, at the dawning?
   A in total eclipse
   B waning in the East
   C in brightest array
   D in the 7th house
   E out the car window   {85% correct on the Internet}

8. "DIZZY" BY TOMMY ROE - It was love at first sight it seems, for Tommy. His head is spinning and he needs to call a doctor for some help! In the beginning of the song, he has a hard time talking to this spellbinder. Why?
   A there's fellas hanging around her all the time
   B she won't look his way
   C he's so shy
   D her current boy friend is awfully big, and kind of strong
   E she hates his guts   {53% correct on the Internet}

9. "CRYSTAL BLUE PERSUASION" BY TOMMY JAMES & THE SHONDELLS - Did you ever try to figure out just what "crystal blue persuasion" might be? It seems to be some sort of a dawning of a new and better age (age of Aquarius?). Anyway, what does Tommy say it is?
   A a fine creation
   B a sweet salvation
   C a self-examination
   D a peaceful incantation
   E a new vibration   {57% correct on the Internet}

10. "TAKE A LETTER MARIA" BY R.B. GREAVES - R.B. (nephew of Sam Cooke), has a problem. Maria, his secretary, needs to take this letter because R.B. won't be going home to his cheating wife anymore. According to the song, who was to get a copy of the letter?
    A his mother
    B his agent
    C his lawyer
    D his circular file
    E no one (needs to know)   {63% correct on the Internet}

11. "JIMMY MACK" BY MARTHA & THE VANDELLAS - We don't know where Jimmy went, but this other guy is calling Martha three times a day. We never find out if the interloper's persistence pays, but we are told that he.....
    A smiles like Jimmy
    B sings the same love songs
    C looks like a prince

D talks as sweet as Jimmy
E has muscles galore   {54% correct on the Internet}

12. "GET ON UP" BY THE ESQUIRES - Almost a one-hit wonder, they followed this one with a minor hit called And Get Away. The singer wants his girl to dance. He mentions the Monkey, Jerk and Shing-a-ling once, but mentions one dance twice. Get on up and.....
   A Swim
   B Boogaloo
   C Electric Slide
   D Funky Chicken
   E Hustle   {68% correct on the Internet}

13. "TIGHTEN UP" BY ARCHIE BELL & THE DRELLS - Don't ask what a "Drell" is, we don't know. We do know that they could really "tighten up", though. This song is unique, because Archie tells us where the group is from, right at the beginning. The location?
   A Memphis, Tennessee
   B Houston, Texas
   C Atlanta, Georgia
   D Pierre, South Dakota
   E Tallahassee, Florida   {38% correct on the Internet}

14. "(SITTIN' ON) THE DOCK OF THE BAY" BY OTIS REDDING - So Otis moved from Georgia and found out that things were pretty much the same in California. He's watching the tide roll away and pretty much killing time. What does he say won't leave him alone?
   A this loneliness
   B the Shore Patrol
   C the blues
   D the sea gulls
   E his yearning for home   {79% correct on the Internet}

15. "FUN, FUN, FUN" BY THE BEACH BOYS - She's in her T-Bird and having fun. The guys can't catch her, and apparently the police can't either. Only her daddy taking the car away will put an end to this foolishness. Where did she tell him she was going?
   A shopping
   B to the malt shop

   C to the library
   D Susie's house
   E Vancouver   {82% correct on the Internet}

16. "IT'S YOUR THING" BY THE ISLEY BROTHERS - Ah, freedom. It seems everyone was made free by the late sixties and we were allowed to do anything that we wished.....free love and all that. So, finish the line....."do what you want to do. I can't tell you".....
   A what's right for you
   B where to rendezvous
   C who to sock it to
   D doobee, doobee, doo
   E when to pay your dues   {65% correct on the Internet}

17. "ONLY THE STRONG SURVIVE" BY JERRY BUTLER - The "Ice Man" had a very tough time when his first love affair ended. He found out that he had to get up off his knees and overcome all the trouble life will give. Where did he get this sage advice?
   A his minister
   B the Bible
   C in a dream
   D his warden
   E his mother   {45% correct on the Internet}

18. "SLOOP JOHN B" BY THE BEACH BOYS - Based on a West Indies folk song, this tune tells of a voyage filled with misfortune. When the first mate got drunk and broke into the captain's trunk, the constable had to come and get him. The constable's name?
   A Mr. Custer
   B Deputy Fife
   C Jackson Brand
   D Sheriff John Stone
   E Officer Brown   {68% correct on the Internet}

19. "FOR WHAT IT'S WORTH" BY BUFFALO SPRINGFIELD - This song became a sort of "anthem" for the youth movement of the 60s. The question is what the guys say strikes deep, and will creep into your life?
   A police brutality
   B drugs
   C paranoia
   D love, sweet, love
   E indecision   {67% correct on the Internet}

20. "TOWN WITHOUT PITY" BY GENE PITNEY - This song expresses rebellion and the angst of two young lovers. They warn that something must be done before "this gray and granite planet falls apart". According to Gene, what is tearing the lovers in two?
   A jealousy
   B petty rules
   C little minds
   D evil ways
   E fickle feelings   {48% correct on the Internet}

GAME 10 - THE PSYCHEDELIC 60s

So many groovy songs, so much harmony, so much hair, so much of everything, it's blowing my mind!

1. Far out, man, let's start with Scott McKenzie, singing his 1967 hit SAN FRANCISCO (BE SURE TO WEAR FLOWERS IN YOUR HAIR). Yes, summertime will be a love-in there and who might you expect to meet there......?
   A messengers of love
   B people without flowers in their hair
   C Colin O'Brien and Dylan Murphy
   D some gentle people   {75% correct on the Internet}

2. Now, we are going to sock it to you with a big 1967 hit from the high-flying Jefferson Airplane, the oft-played SOMEBODY TO LOVE. Yes, you do, when the truth is found to be lies, and you are so bummed-out that your friends treat you like.....?
   A you're over 30
   B a guest
   C you have a goiter
   D Richard Nixon   {81% correct on the Internet}

3. Procul Harum really put us in a groovy mood with the offbeat A WHITER SHADE OF PALE, which was based on a cantata by Bach. Solemn and mysterious, this 1967 hit with strange lyrics mentions 16 vestal virgins. Exactly, where were they going.....?
   A leaving for the coast
   B up on the roof
   C to a cabin in the woods
   D San Francisco   {83% correct on the Internet}

4. Steppenwolf expressed the freedom of the late 60s with BORN TO BE WILD, a 1968 hit. The song mentions "heavy-metal" thunder, which may have been the birth of that musical term. Complete the line "fire all of your guns at once and.....
   A sock it to me, baby"
   B explode into space"

C do me a solid"
   D leave the human race"   {89% correct on the Internet}

5. Now, let's get high with Donovan and his HURDY-GURDY MAN, which made it to No. 5 in 1968. By the way, a hurdy-gurdy is defined as a lute-shaped barrel organ (so there!). Anyway, according to the song, what did the HG-Man do.....?
   A he came singing songs of love
   B he stole raisins
   C he touched the sky
   D he played knick-knack paddy-whack   {74% correct on the Internet}

6. The 1969 album Crosby, Stills & Nash was a high-point for hippies (and others) that year. MARRAKESH EXPRESS wasn't a big seller on the charts, but it is heard often today. Complete the line, "I've been saving all my money just to take you there.....
   A we'll get the cashmere at the fair"
   B we'll pay everybody's fare"
   C I smell the garden in your hair"
   D and where we stop, I don't care"   {54% correct on the Internet}

7. Hey, man, we're going to Woodstock, where The Jefferson Airplane sang their 1967 hit, WHITE RABBIT. Excuse me, while I kiss the sky....is this song about drugs or, what? According to this song, which pills don't do anything at all.....?
   A the ones from the Pez dispenser
   B the green ones
   C the ones from the candy man
   D the ones that your mother gives you {79% correct on the Internet}

8. Another song which helped set the mood of the times was the 1967 hit FOR WHAT IT'S WORTH (STOP, HEY WHAT'S THAT SOUND), by The Buffalo Springfield. According to this song, protesting people carried signs which mostly said what.....?
   A Hooray For Our Side!
   B We're Living In A Society!
   C Don't Trust Anyone Over 30!
   D Right On!   {75% correct on the Internet}

9. In 1969, The Youngbloods had a gold record with GET TOGETHER. This mellow song kind of explained how we all could bring peace to this crazy world. You may have peace of mind if you can pick out the first two lines of this song.....
   A "Everything is beautiful, in its own way"
   B "Listen to me, these pretzels are making me thirsty"
   C "It's the time of the season, for loving"
   D "Love is but a song we sing, fear's the way we die"   {68% correct on the Internet}

10. Mellow, man! We're back in 1965.....far out! It's The Byrds, who helped start this groovy music scene. Wow, they're singing MR. TAMBOURINE MAN! It's all hazy, but the singer is asking the T-Man to take him for a trip upon.....?
   A his magic loogie tip
   B his magic swirling ship
   C his magic black roach clip
   D his magic johnson   {96% correct on the Internet}

11. Wait, it's only a few months later and The Byrds suddenly seem to have it all together with TURN! TURN! TURN! (TO EVERYTHING THERE IS A SEASON). This mellow, but philosophical song has which of the following origins.....?
   A music by Yo Yo Ma, words from Death of a Salesman
   B music by Woody Guthrie, words from the Kama Sutra
   C music by Pete Seeger, words from the Bible
   D music by Bob Dylan, words from the Koran   {74% correct on the Internet}

12. The biggest hit for The Rascals was their hit from 1968 called PEOPLE GOT TO BE FREE. It stayed at No. 1 for five weeks! They say that we all need to learn to live together and love one another. To do so, the singer says it seems.....
   A we've got to get it on
   B we got to say, "not that there's anything wrong with that"
   C we got to start it individually
   D we've got to follow the golden rule   {69% correct on the Internet}

13. When we talk about protest music, it's probably wise to include the Kingston Trio. Back in 1962, they hit it big with the anti-war WHERE HAVE ALL THE FLOWERS GONE. According to this song, where have all the flowers gone.....?
   A maybe the dingo ate your flowers
   B crushed by warfare, all of them
   C young girls picked them, everyone
   D gone to graveyards, everyone   {43% correct on the Internet}

14. In 1965, Barry McGuire made it to No. 1 with EVE OF DESTRUCTION, a protest song which pulled no punches. In fact, it's still a pretty good history lesson. I don't know how we have survived, but he said that even the Jordan River had.....
   A bodies floatin'
   B uromysitisis poisoning
   C too much pollution
   D naval warfare   {79% correct on the Internet}

15. In 1968, Eric Burdon & The Animals had a hit with the anti-war SKY PILOT (PART ONE). Although his job title was never actually stated in the song, it was clear what the Sky Pilot's duty was in the war zone. He was a......?
   A medic
   B minister
   C quone
   D anti-aircraft gunner   {46% correct on the Internet}

16. In 1969, one-hit wonders Zager & Evans gave us a somber look at the future with the hit IN THE YEAR 2525 (EXORDIUM & TERMINUS), which was No. 1 for six weeks! In the year 6565, where would people pick their sons and daughters from.....?
   A somewhere in space
   B a computer
   C at the nearest flea market
   D the bottom of a long glass tube   {77% correct on the Internet}

17. In 1967, singer/songwriter Janis Ian had her first hit with a song called SOCIETY'S CHILD (BABY I'VE BEEN THINKING). She wrote this song at 14, about an ill-fated romance. She couldn't see her boyfriend anymore because.....
  A he lived in a bubble
  B he was poor
  C he was black
  D he was too old   {58% correct on the Internet}

18. In 1968, Dion (originally with the Belmonts) had his last rock hit with ABRAHAM, MARTIN AND JOHN. This nice song with the harp sounds throughout was a tribute to Lincoln, Martin Luther King, JFK and one other person.....
  A Willie Mays
  B Bobby Kennedy
  C Franklin Roosevelt
  D Mahatma Gandhi   {76% correct on the Internet}

19. Even though the protest song WAR by Edwin Starr is from 1970, we figure that's close enough to the 60s. Edwin tells us that war is a friend to one person only, the.....
  A gravedigger
  B devil
  C undertaker
  D dark and disturbed   {74% correct on the Internet}

20. Far out! And, since we're stretching our self-imposed rules, let's finish with the 1971 hit SIGNS by the Five Man Electrical Band, sort of a summary of the hippie attitude. At the beginning of the song, which people do they say need not apply for a job.....?
  A anyone over 30
  B long-haired, freaky people
  C Moops
  D young people   {89% correct on the Internet}

Chapter 2 - From the 60s to the 70s

GAME 1 - LYRICAL BITS FROM THE 60s AND 70s

Turn off the radio and concentrate. These are lyrical hints from one or more songs by a popular artist. You pick the artist.....

1. He left his sleeping bag behind the couch, and he heard voices in the wires.
   A Barry Manilow
   B Neil Diamond
   C Glen Campbell
   D Elton John   {71% correct on the Internet}

2. He was "a little too tall," he stood on the corner at midnight working on his courage, and he was running "8 miles a minute"
   A James Taylor
   B Neil Young
   C Kenny Rogers
   D Bob Seger   {90% correct on the Internet}

3. In an early hit, he would go out late at night and "chug-a-lug and shout." In a later hit he wondered if he would see his little boy in heaven.
   A Roger Williams
   B Rod Stewart
   C Eric Clapton
   D John Denver   {93% correct on the Internet}

4. This group sang about nights that were "stronger than moonshine," heat that was hot (maybe after the moonshine?), sharing the gift of gab, and being a poor correspondent
   A Lynyrd Skynyrd
   B Crosby Stills and Nash
   C America
   D The Eagles
   E Hall & Oates   {62% correct on the Internet}

5. Who went looking for romance at the dance? And thought that girls from the east were "hip"? And sang about the girl that told her dad she was going to the library and then took off in the fancy car?
   A Beach Boys
   B Lionel Ritchie
   C Michael Jackson
   D Rupert Holmes   {97% correct on the Internet}

6. He sang about a wishing box, a faded number on a matchbook, and a razor hidden in a shoe.
   A Barry Manilow
   B Jim Croce
   C Billy Joel
   D Harry Chapin   {85% correct on the Internet}

7. Who sang about purple berries, a lady in lace lamenting her lost love, and a youthful crowd of a half-million?
   A Carole King
   B Judy Collins
   C Crosby, Stills, and Nash
   D Peter, Paul, and Mary   {72% correct on the Internet}

8. Songs from this person or group were about happy fishes in the sea, a black child and a white child, and a comparison between heaven and Oklahoma
   A John Denver
   B Creedence Clearwater Revival
   C Three Dog Night
   D Bob Seger
   E Kenny Rogers   {80% correct on the Internet}

9. L.A. fog, flying from Miami Beach to Russia, 4000 holes, and Edgar Allan Poe.
   A The Beatles
   B The Rolling Stones
   C Elton John
   D Phil Collins   {83% correct on the Internet}

10. He or she knew about Hollywood and Redwood and north Ontario, and told us what it's like to be 24 years old.
   A Cher
   B Gordon Lightfoot
   C Dionne Warwick
   D Neil Young   {76% correct on the Internet}

11. He/she/they sang about jet planes, lemon trees, hammers, and magic dragons.
   A Cher
   B Peter Paul & Mary
   C Jackie DeShannon
   D Donovan
   E The Haskes   {89% correct on the Internet}

12. This lady's best-known album and its title song told of blue and gold bits of magic woven together.
   A Whitney Houston
   B Thelma Houston
   C Judy Collins
   D Barbra Streisand
   E Carole King   {73% correct on the Internet}

13. Their most popular song had a connection with a Christian association for young men.
   A Beatles
   B Village People
   C Paul Simon
   D Bob Dylan
   E Beach Boys   {91% correct on the Internet}

14. The singer may be seeing double with a 103-degree fever, but would climb a mountain and sail across the sea for someone who was icy cold
   A Foreigner
   B Genesis
   C 5th Dimension
   D Temptations   {89% correct on the Internet}

15. Take care if you come near his back stairs -- or you'll be like a paperback novel in the gales of November...
   A Billy Joel
   B Phil Collins
   C Gordon Lightfoot
   D Paul Simon
   E John Lennon   {82% correct on the Internet}

16. To the Memphis queen loaded with gin -- pleased to meetchoo:
   A Rolling Stones
   B Bob Dylan
   C Beatles
   D Elton John
   E Rod Stewart   {84% correct on the Internet}

17. The singer tries and tries and tries and tries, but life's unkind and getting old is a drag...
   A Rolling Stones
   B Bob Dylan
   C Beatles
   D Elton John
   E Rod Stewart   {80% correct on the Internet}

18. The singer said there's too many brothers dying and too many mothers crying.
   A Sly and the Family Stone
   B The Doors
   C Jimi Hendrix
   D Marvin Gaye
   E Tennessee Ernie Ford   {92% correct on the Internet}

19. Minute by minute the catfish are jumping and the paddle wheel is pumping, but we the people need a way to make us smile.
   A Tina Turner
   B Linda Ronstadt
   C Carole King
   D Everly Brothers
   E Doobie Brothers   {83% correct on the Internet}

20. He sang about sunshine and moonshine and sunny days that he thought would never end -- how sweet it is!
   A Bill Withers
   B Neil Young
   C John Denver
   D James Taylor
   E Bruce Springsteen   {88% correct on the Internet}

GAME 2 - 70s WHO - WHAT - WHERE

Some of these are a bit tough. But you remember them, don't you?

1. The singer met her in a club in Old Soho, where "girls will be boys, and boys will be girls"...WHO?
   A Caribbean Queen by Billy Ocean
   B Lady In Red by Chris DeBurgh
   C Lady Marmalade by LaBelle
   D Layla by Derek and the Dominos
   E Lola by the Kinks   {86% correct on the Internet}

2. He knew Paul, the real estate novelist (whatever that is), Davy from the Navy, and an old man who really loved his tonic and gin...WHO?
   A The Village People's Macho Man
   B Billy Joel's Piano Man
   C Bread's Guitar Man
   D Kenny Rogers' Gambler   {88% correct on the Internet}

3. Down by the corner, about a half mile from here...Miss Lucy was down by the tracks; she lost her home and her family and she won't be coming back...on WHAT?
   A Long Train Running by the Doobie Brothers
   B Peace Train by Cat Stevens
   C Love Train by the O'Jays
   D Last Train To Clarksville by the Monkees
   E Morning Train by Sheena Easton   {72% correct on the Internet}

4. There's a killer out there, and his brain is making toad-like movements. If you give him a ride, you will lose your memory...WHO?
   A Gypsy Man by War
   B Desperado by the Eagles
   C Renegade by Styx
   D Riders On The Storm by the Doors
   E Typical Male by Tina Turner   {70% correct on the Internet}

5. Friday night, late…Glenn Miller's band…the Porter tunes…During all this, the singer was doing WHAT?
   A Standing in the Shadows of Love by the Four Tops
   B Dreamin' by Johnny Burnette
   C Reminiscing by The Little River Band
   D Smokin' In The Boy's Room by Brownsville Station   {64% correct on the Internet}

6. On his way to very good things, the singer found some wings…"distant roads" were calling him…he changed like the seasons, and you needn't wonder why…This all happens WHEN?
   A No Time by the Guess Who
   B Beginnings by Chicago
   C It's Now Or Never by Elvis Presley
   D When Doves Cry by Prince
   E Sweet Seasons by Carole King   {65% correct on the Internet}

7. Ooh, baby, your face is "mellow as the month of May." The singer can't stand it when he/she is looked at that way…WHY?
   A Anticipation by Carly Simon
   B I Feel The Earth Move by Carole King
   C Feels Like The First Time by Foreigner
   D Feel Like Makin' Love by Bad Company
   E More Than A Feeling by Boston   {52% correct on the Internet}

8. Everybody's talking about revolution and evolution…Hare Krishna…this-ism, that-ism. WHY?
   A Freedom by Wham!
   B Gonna Fly Now by Bill Conti
   C Fly Like An Eagle by Steve Miller
   D Revolution by the Beatles
   E Give Peace A Chance by John Lennon   {57% correct on the Internet}

9. It "makes you feel happy, like an old-time movie"…it might be jug band music or R&B or rock and roll. WHAT?
   A. Do You Believe In Magic by the Lovin' Spoonful
   B. Sweet Soul Music by Arthur Conley
   C. Dance, Dance, Dance by the Beach Boys

D. Dancin' In The Street by Martha and the Vandellas
   E. Moonlight Feels Right by Starbuck {57% correct on the Internet}

10. There was a showgirl with yellow feathers in her hair and a low-cut dress. She would do the merengue and the cha-cha...WHERE?
   A. On Broadway by the Drifters
   B. Walk On The Wild Side by Lou Reed
   C. Copacabana by Barry Manilow
   D. Rock The Casbah by the Clash   {88% correct on the Internet}

11. In "this ever changing world in which we live in," you've got to "give the other fellow hell!" HOW OR WHY?
   A Kung Fu Fighting by Carl Douglas
   B Bang A Gong by T. Rex
   C Live And Let Die by Paul McCartney
   D Coward Of The County by Kenny Rogers   {84% correct on the Internet}

12. The singer will meet you at the station. The reservation was made for 4:30. The singer asks you not to be slow -- and he/she doesn't know if he/she is ever coming home. On WHAT?
   A Long Train Running by the Doobie Brothers
   B Peace Train by Cat Stevens
   C Love Train by the O'Jays
   D Last Train To Clarksville by the Monkees
   E Morning Train by Sheena Easton   {63% correct on the Internet}

13. The singer and the subject of this question were both "too tired to sleep"...the latter was given the last of the bottle and a cigarette, and he told the singer that he had to know when to walk away (maybe when someone's mooching your booze and smokes!)....WHO?
   A Mr. Bojangles by the Nitty Gritty Dirt Band
   B Mr. Blue by the Fleetwoods
   C Gypsy Man by War
   D Ramblin' Gamblin' Man by Bob Seger
   E The Gambler by Kenny Rogers   {76% correct on the Internet}

14. An unusual girl, an unusual name. They danced together under the moon. But "where was June?" The singer never knew her, but he loved her name. WHO?
   A Angelia by Richard Marx
   B Aubrey by Bread
   C Glendora by Perry Como
   D Patches by Dickey Lee
   E Windy by the Association   {43% correct on the Internet}

15. The children at your feet wonder how you manage to make ends meet. The baby at your breast wonders how you manage to feed the rest. WHO?
   A Lady Madonna by the Beatles
   B Gypsy Woman by Brian Hyland
   C Patches by Dickey Lee
   D Proud Mary by Creedence Clearwater Revival
   E Clean Up Woman by Betty Wright   {85% correct on the Internet}

16. The singer saw her picture and her name in lights. This was her big debut - a dream come true. So he asks her to smile for the camera. WHO?
   A Peg by Steely Dan
   B Sheila by Tommy Roe
   C Sunny by Bobbie Hebb
   D Long Cool Woman by the Hollies
   E Long Tall Sally by Little Richard   {63% correct on the Internet}

17. The singer thinks the girl is afraid of what he might have on his mind. But he says he'll take good care of her if she'll accept his love. Wonder if she fell for it. WHO?
   A Come On Eileen by Dexys Midnight Runners
   B Hey Paula by Paul & Paula
   C Sweet Love by the Commodores
   D Lady by Kenny Rogers
   E Lady Willpower by Gary Puckett and the Union Gap   {50% correct on the Internet}

18. He kisses them and loves them because they're all pretty much the same to him. He hugs them and squeezes them, even if they don't know his name. WHO is this sexist guy?
   A Handy Man by Jimmy Jones
   B Duke of Earl by Gene Chandler
   C The Wanderer by Dion
   D The Rapper by Jaggerz   {85% correct on the Internet}

19. He wonders where you are and what you do. He wonders if you're feeling lonely. He has no idea how to win your heart. But he makes a good start by saying he loves you. WHY?
   A Never Can Say Goodbye by the Jackson 5
   B Baby Come Back by Player
   C Hello by Lionel Richie
   D Hello Again by Neil Diamond
   E Hello It's Me by Todd Rundgren   {72% correct on the Internet}

20. In his mind, the singer has "sunshine on a cloudy day" and "the month of May." WHAT makes him feel this way?
   A Sweet Love by the Commodores
   B Everlasting Love by Andy Gibb
   C My Love by Paul McCartney
   D My Girl by the Temptations
   E Sweet Little Sixteen by Chuck Berry   {88% correct on the Internet}

GAME 3 - BITS & PIECES FROM THE 60s AND 70s

Can you name that tune with a few hints? If so, that should help your score.

1. Someone in the song really likes peaches, and therefore wants to shake a tree.
   A Karma Chameleon by the Culture Club
   B Yummy Yummy Yummy by the Ohio Express
   C Strange Magic by the Electric Light Orchestra
   D The Joker by the Steve Miller Band   {85% correct on the Internet}

2. She wears blue jeans, comes from L.A., and is a seamstress for the band.
   A Tiny Dancer by Elton John
   B Angie by the Rolling Stones
   C Angie Baby by Helen Reddy
   D Lady Madonna by the Beatles   {73% correct on the Internet}

3. The singer and this person were "hitchin' on a twilight train"
   A Sundown by Gordon Lightfoot
   B The Most Beautiful Girl by Charlie Rich
   C Cracklin' Rosie by Neil Diamond
   D Maggie May by Rod Stewart   (70% correct on the Internet}

4. Someone in this song has plans to make another person blue. I'll bet you wonder how I knew!
   A Careless Whisper by Wham!
   B Sounds of Silence by Simon and Garfunkle
   C I Heard a Rumor by Bananarama
   D I Heard It Through the Grapevine by Marvin Gaye   {76% correct on the Internet}

5. It was so easy when the other person was "light and breezy."
   A You Don't Bring Me Flowers by Barbra Streisand and Neil Diamond
   B With or Without You by U2

   C It's Too Late by Carole King
   D Don't Leave Me This Way by Thelma Houston   {57% correct on the Internet}

6. The singer is up and gone by 5 in the morning -- lawdy, how long did it go on?
   A The Chain Gang by Sam Cooke
   B Sixteen Tons by Tennessee Ernie Ford
   C Folsom Prison Blues by Johnny Cash
   D Take This Job and Shove It by Johnny Paycheck
   E Working in the Coal Mine by Lee Dorsey   {62% correct on the Internet}

7. This song tells us about paranoia. It creeps into your life, but then goes deep inside. You're always afraid, but if you mess up they'll come take you away.
   A Back Stabbers by the O'Jays
   B Lowdown by Boz Scaggs
   C Don't Fear The Reaper by Blue Oyster Cult
   D For What It's Worth by Buffalo Springfield   {45% correct on the Internet}

8. A certain 'spirit' was last seen here in 1969
   A Carefree Highway by Gordon Lightfoot
   B Copacabana by Barry Manilow
   C Psychedelic Shack by the Temptations
   D Hotel California by the Eagles
   E Woodstock by Crosby, Stills, Nash, and Young   {78% correct on the Internet}

9. The singer tells an unwanted suitor to take a long, long vacation
   A My Boyfriend's Back by the Angels
   B The Bitch Is Back by Elton John
   C We Are Family by Sister Sledge
   D Run For Your Life by the Beatles   {74% correct on the Internet}

10. "Who do you think you are?"
   A Mr. Big Stuff by Jean Knight
   B She Works Hard for the Money by Donna Summer

   C Superstar by the Carpenters
   D Devil Woman by Cliff Richard   {58% correct on the Internet}

11. Where the birds are out of tune and you can't see the moon because of all the clouds:
   A (In) Margaritaville by Jimmy Buffett
   B (On) Blueberry Hill by Fats Domino
   C A World Without Love by Peter and Gordon
   D Down By The Old Mill (Stream) by Arthur Clough   {78% correct on the Internet}

12. She was tall, well-tanned, young, and very lovely.
   A Diana by Paul Anka
   B Donna by Ritchie Valens
   C The Girl From Ipanema by Stan Getz and Astrud Gilberto
   D The Most Beautiful Girl by Charlie Rich
   E Long Cool Woman by the Hollies   {61% correct on the Internet}

13. The singer was walking in the rain, crying, feeling a pain, and wishing that his girl could help end his misery.
   A Runaway by Del Shannon
   B Runaround Sue by Dion
   C I Want You Back by the Jackson 5
   D You're The One That I Want by John Travolta and Olivia Newton-John
   E Alone Again (Naturally) by Gilbert O'Sullivan   {61% correct on the Internet}

14. We are informed that there are 1,352 guitar pickers and 16,821 mothers associated with this song.
   A Memphis by Johnny Rivers
   B Walking In Memphis by Marc Cohn
   C Nashville Cats by the Lovin' Spoonful
   D Rock And Roll Heaven by the Righteous Brothers
   E Dueling Banjos by Eric Weissberg and Steve Mandell   {40% correct on the Internet}

15. Meteorological factoid. This song tells us all about the rain in Indianapolis in the summertime.
   A Tie A Yellow Ribbon Round The Ole Oak Tree by Dawn
   B Little Green Apples by O. C. Smith
   C Ode To Billie Joe by Bobbie Gentry
   D Purple Haze by Jimi Hendrix   {70% correct on the Internet}

16. What song do these words come from? puppet...poet...pawn...pauper...pirate
   A Karma Chameleon by the Culture Club
   B Atlantis by Donovan
   C That's Life by Frank Sinatra
   D Man In The Mirror by Michael Jackson   {64% correct on the Internet}

17. The singer thinks he may be crucified, so he appeals to Christ.
   A King Of Pain by the Police
   B Running On Empty by Jackson Browne
   C Ballad Of John And Yoko by the Beatles
   D Died In Your Arms by Cutting Crew   {69% correct on the Internet}

18. This came to be at Yasgur's Farm
   A Spirit In The Sky by Norman Greenbaum
   B We're An American Band by Grand Funk
   C Woodstock by Crosby, Stills, Nash, and Young
   D Everyday People by Sly And The Family Stone   {80% correct on the Internet}

19. A cynical attitude maybe, but whether in your car or playing your guitar they'll still "stone you."
   A White Rabbit by Jefferson Airplane
   B Rainy Day Women # 12 & 35 by Bob Dylan
   C Marrakesh Express by Crosby, Stills, and Nash
   D Mother's Little Helper by the Rolling Stones   {71% correct on the Internet}

20. This song goes on about flag wavers, the red white and blue, and 'hail to the chief.'
   A Fortunate Son by Creedence Clearwater Revival
   B We're An American Band by Grand Funk
   C Philadelphia Freedom by Elton John
   D Back Stabbers by the O'Jays   {65% correct on the Internet}

GAME 4 - BEATLES I

If you think you know the songs of the Fab Four, here's your chance to check.

1. The Beatles' first hit, written when the boys were in (or taking a day off from) high school.
    A Please Please Me
    B I Want to Hold Your Hand
    C She Loves You
    D Love Me Do   {37% correct on the Internet}

2. "Get Back," "Yesterday," and "Fool on the Hill" were all written and sung (and left-hand strummed) by:
    A John
    B Paul
    C George
    D Ringo   {86% correct on the Internet}

3. "Come Together," "I Feel Fine," and "Strawberry Fields Forever" were all written and sung by:
    A John
    B Paul
    C George
    D Ringo   {82% correct on the Internet}

4. She was one of "all the lonely people":
    A Lady Madonna
    B Michelle
    C Eleanor Rigby
    D Miss Scarlett   {92% correct on the Internet}

5. Which song was not sung by Ringo?
    A Yellow Submarine
    B Octopus's Garden
    C Hey Jude
    D With a Little Help from My Friends   {88% correct on the Internet}

6. The song in which the Beatles complain about "working like a dog":
   A Paperback Writer
   B Carry that Weight
   C Fixing a Hole
   D A Hard Day's Night   {97% correct on the Internet}

7. A toughie. "Hold your head up, you silly girl," were Paul's words to his dog (who perhaps had an accident?). The song was:
   A Martha My Dear
   B Julia
   C Michelle
   D Dear Prudence   {62% correct on the Internet}

8. Which of these unique terms was NOT in "Come Together"? (It was in "I am the Walrus," where it was dripping from... oh, never mind)
   A Mojo filter
   B Joo Joo eyeball
   C Yellow matter custard
   D Toe jam football   {85% correct on the Internet}

9. The song "I am the Walrus" mentions this famous (and quaint and curious) person:
   A Edgar Allen Poe
   B Queen Elizabeth
   C Julius Caesar
   D O. J. Simpson   {77% correct on the Internet}

10. This is what Rocky Raccoon found when he fell back into his room. He needed it.
   A A bible
   B A gun
   C Lill (Nancy) McGill
   D A message on his answering machine   {70% correct on the Internet}

11. What the Beatles said about dancing to the songs of your grandparents:
   A You Can't Do That
   B It Won't Be Long
   C I'll Cry Instead
   D Why Don't We Do it in the Road
   E Your Mother Should Know   {56% correct on the Internet}

12. Not a George Harrison composition (it's not his style):
   A Something
   B While My Guitar Gently Weeps
   C Here Comes the Sun
   D Revolution   {82% correct on the Internet}

13. The Fool on the Hill had this. Not as peaceful as you thought up there.
   A Tears in his eyes
   B A thousand voices
   C A curious smile
   D IBM stock   {68% correct on the Internet}

14. Which "colorful" word was not used in a Beatles song title:
   A yellow
   B purple
   C golden
   D blues   {73% correct on the Internet}

15. Here's an acronymic clue for you all: Brian Epstein At The London England Show. Sort of an "association" question.
   A Strawberry Fields Forever
   B Lucy in the Sky with Diamonds
   C Yellow Submarine
   D Revolution   {71% correct on the Internet}

16. Eleanor Rigby apparently spent a lot of time:
   A in a church
   B in a bar
   C in drag
   D with Fr. McKenzie   {75% correct on the Internet}

17. Polythene Pam (she's so good lookin' but...) apparently spent a lot of time:
   A in a church
   B in a bar
   C in drag
   D with Fr. McKenzie   {63% correct on the Internet}

18. Which was not considered as "proof" that Paul was dead?
   A A shoeless Paul on the Abbey Road album cover
   B The line "he blew his mind out in a car" from "A Day in the Life"
   C The words "is he dead?" at the end of "I am the Walrus"
   D Silly Love Songs   {77% correct on the Internet}

19. This "animal" song has foggy L.A. as its setting. Please don't be long with the answer.
   A I Am the Walrus
   B Little Piggies
   C Octopus's Garden
   D Rocky Raccoon
   E Blue Jay Way   {51% correct on the Internet}

20. The most depressing Beatles song, as measured by the singer being lied to, laughed at, and moaned about, and having his gifts thrown away. You'd be in the dumps, too.
   A While My Guitar Gently Weeps
   B I'm a Loser
   C I'm Down
   D Yer Blues
   E I'll Cry Instead   {39% correct on the Internet}

GAME 5 - BEATLES II

Here's another game of all Beatles' songs.....are you surprised?

1. A song that was popularized by the Beatles and then again by the movie "Ferris Bueller's Day Off":
   A She's a Woman
   B I Want to Hold Your Hand
   C A Hard Day's Night
   D Twist and Shout   {77% correct on the Internet}

2. Which very "moving" song describes a "Sunday driver"? (It took me so long to find out, but I found out.)
   A Drive My Car
   B Ticket to Ride
   C Day Tripper
   D Run for Your Life
   E Helter Skelter   {73% correct on the Internet}

3. This song describes someone who is NOT depraved, destitute, destructive, or desperate:
   A Maxwell's Silver Hammer
   B Rocky Raccoon
   C Bungalow Bill
   D Michelle
   E Lady Madonna   {70% correct on the Internet}

4. The only instrumental by the Beatles:
   A Blue Jay Way
   B Golden Slumbers
   C Revolution #9
   D Flying   {47% correct on the Internet}

5. This job title did NOT appear in a Beatles song title:
   A Undertaker
   B Doctor
   C Writer
   D Taxman   {62% correct on the Internet}

6. Which of these "money" songs was not done by the Beatles:
   A Baby You're a Rich Man
   B Can't Buy Me Love
   C You Never Give Me Your Money
   D Penny Lover   {76% correct on the Internet}

7. A rather unpleasant Beatles association. Only one of these songs was not referred to by Charles Manson during his bloody rampage. Which one?
   A Helter Skelter
   B Little Piggies
   C Revolution #9
   D Maxwell's Silver Hammer   {56% correct on the Internet}

8. Maxwell (who was majoring in medicine) used his silver hammer to dispose of everyone except:
   A A friend named Joan
   B A teacher
   C A preacher
   D A judge   {48% correct on the Internet}

9. One was glass, one was honey, one was savoy, one was mean, but only one was a food not mentioned in a Beatles song title:
   A pie
   B onion
   C mustard
   D crumpet
   E truffle   {55% correct on the Internet}

10. In "Glass Onion," there was a clue for you all about "I Am The Walrus." Who was the walrus?
   A John
   B Paul
   C George
   D Ringo
   E Yoko   {63% correct on the Internet}

11. Which did not appear in "Lucy in the Sky with Diamonds"?
   A Rocking-horse people
   B Plasticine porters
   C Newspaper taxis
   D Gingerbread judges
   E Tangerine trees   {73% correct on the Internet}

12. Which of these events/occasions is just "waiting to take you away"?
   A Magical Mystery Tour
   B Birthday
   C Revolution
   D (For) the Benefit of Mr. Kite   {90% correct on the Internet}

13. In "I'm So Tired," whom did the Beatles curse during their bout of insomnia?
   A Neighbors playing loud Rolling Stones music
   B Jack Daniels
   C Sir Walter Raleigh
   D Mrs. Folger   {52% correct on the Internet}

14. The Beatles' helpful advice in "times of trouble":
   A Think for Yourself
   B Wait
   C Let It Be
   D We Can Work It Out   {88% correct on the Internet}

15. This song describes a time when "my troubles seemed so far away":
   A Birthday
   B Yesterday
   C The Night Before
   D A Hard Day's Night
   E 8 Days a Week   {95% correct on the Internet}

16. Which one cannot be found in "Penny Lane"?
   A Barber showing photographs
   B Doctor with a boutonniere
   C Banker with a motorcar
   D Fireman with an hourglass   {78% correct on the Internet}

17. What was the big complaint in "I'm a Loser"?
   A Ringo was singing
   B The money was all gone
   C A girl in a million was lost
   D A true love couldn't be found   {57% correct on the Internet}

18. "Yellow Submarine" was, according to a later revelation by the Beatles, a
   A Song about drugs
   B Song with sexual references
   C Song about the absurdity of war
   D Song for kids   {51% correct on the Internet}

19. "No one, I think, is of the same mind as me. I must be a genius or a madman." This paraphrases which John Lennon song:
   A Revolution
   B Come Together
   C Strawberry Fields Forever
   D Hard Day's Night   {52% correct on the Internet}

20. "Hey Jude" was written by Paul McCartney for
   A Julian Lennon (when his parents, John and Cynthia, were breaking up)
   B Judy Collins (to show his affection for her)
   C Judy Garland (of Wizard of Oz fame)
   D Jude (Paul's dog)   {75% correct on the Internet}

GAME 6 - 60s SOUL

These are from the 60s, so be aware that there was peace, love, and...........soul.

1. The first song for this game is I GOT YOU (I FEEL GOOD) from James Brown, "The Godfather of Soul". It was a No. 1 R&B hit for six weeks in 1965. What phrase does James use repeatedly to rhyme with "I feel nice....."?
   A gonna' melt the ice
   B rollin' the dice
   C sugar and spice
   D take my advice   {82% correct on the Internet}

2. In 1965, The Temptations had their first No. 1 song with MY GIRL. It was co-written by Smokey Robinson. In the beginning of the song, what do the Temps say they have "when it's cold outside....."?
   A the summer breeze
   B the month of May
   C burning love
   D the sunshine of your love   {95% correct on the Internet}

3. Also from 1965, The Four Tops had their first No. 1 hit with I CAN'T HELP MYSELF. This Holland-Dozier-Holland composition is sometimes listed with a subtitle, sometimes not. What is this phrase, heard often in the song?
   A Get Down Tonight
   B Baby I Need Your Lovin'
   C Boogety, Boogety, Shoo
   D Sugar Pie, Honey Bunch   {92% correct on the Internet}

4. In 1965 The Supremes had one of their many No. 1 hits with a song called STOP! IN THE NAME OF LOVE. Many times throughout the song, the girls made their request before what would happen.....?
   A before you break my heart
   B you go on down the road

  C before it's all over
  D you go in peace, the song has ended   {100% correct on the Internet}

5. Again in 1965, The Miracles had a very memorable hit with THE TRACKS OF MY TEARS, although it only made it to No. 16 on the pop charts. In this lament for the loss of his girl, what does the singer say is his "makeup" since his breakup?
  A his tissue
  B his smile
  C the darkness
  D sadness   {78% correct on the Internet}

6. Moving on to 1966, when Bobby Hebb had his only hit with SUNNY, which was certified as a gold record. At the beginning of the song, what does the singer say his life was filled with yesterday.....?
  A sunshine, lollipops and rainbows
  B love
  C indecision
  D rain   {81% correct on the Internet}

7. In 1966, The Temptations hit it big again with AIN'T TO PROUD TO BEG, which was a No. 1 R&B hit for eight weeks! Where did the singer say he would sleep all night and day to keep his girl from walking away.....?
  A up on the roof
  B on her doorstep
  C in her backyard
  D under her bed   {87% correct on the Internet}

8. Again in 1966, one-hit wonders The Capitols made it to the No. 7 with COOL JERK. The singer mentions that some guys were looking at him like he was a fool, but, he says, deep down inside, they know.....
  A he's not to be ridiculed
  B he's cool
  C he's a little daft
  D he's outta' sight   {65% correct on the Internet}

9. One more one-hit wonder from 1966. This one was called BAREFOOTIN' and was by Robert Parker. What was the name of the female party-goer who was barefootin' after throwing away her wig and high sneakers.....?

  A Sweet Little Sixteen
  B Hard-Hearted Hannah
  C Long, Tall Sally
  D Bony Moronie   {35% correct on the Internet}

10. On to 1967, when Gladys Knight & The Pips made it to No. 2 with I HEARD IT THROUGH THE GRAPEVINE, which became an even bigger hit for Marvin Gaye in 1968. According to the song, what did she actually hear.....?

  A "not much longer would you be mine"
  B "all you ever do is whine"
  C "our love has no more time"
  D "you're walking on down the line"   {97% correct on the Internet}

11. Also in 1967, Aaron Neville had his first hit with a song called TELL IT LIKE IT IS. In this song, Aaron tells his woman that his time is too expensive and if she wants something to play with, she should.....?

  A play around with someone else
  B go look for a playboy
  C try Toys R Us, already!
  D go and find herself a toy   {71% correct on the Internet}

12. Jackie Wilson hit it big in 1967 with (YOUR LOVE KEEPS LIFTING ME) HIGHER AND HIGHER. In middle of the song, he says he was once downhearted. What does he say was his "closest friend" before she came along.....?

  A cheeseburgers
  B bourbon
  C disappointment
  D loneliness   {61% correct on the Internet}

13. Joe Tex had a gold record in 1967 with SKINNY LEGS AND ALL. It was recorded "live". He is trying to give the lady with the skinny legs away and nobody seems to want her. Who does he end up giving her to.....?
   A Leroy
   B Otis
   C Billy Bob
   D the fiddle player   {37% correct on the Internet}

14. Another one from The Temptations, this one from 1968. It was called CLOUD NINE and made it to No. 6. For better or worse, where do they say a man is when he's on good ol' Cloud Nine.....
   A "on lonely street"
   B "free from life at last"
   C "a million miles from reality"
   D "at a Chicago Cubs World Series game"   {79% correct on the Internet}

15. More Temptations (they WERE once voted America's all-time favorite soul group). In 1968 again, they made it to No. 4 with I WISH IT WOULD RAIN. His girl is gone and his future went with her. Where does he stay day after day.....?
   A at the coffee shop
   B locked up in his room
   C up on the roof
   D in this prison of pain   {46% correct on the Internet}

16. In 1968, Johnny Taylor had his first big hit (he had three), called WHO'S MAKING LOVE. The question is asked who's making love to your old lady, while.....?
   A "you was out making love"
   B "the dice are rollin' all night"
   C "you're doin' your thing"
   D "your old lady is out of town"   {72% correct on the Internet}

17. This big hit for Sly & The Family Stone was No. 1 for four weeks in 1969. It was called EVERYDAY PEOPLE and basically tried to tell us that we are all very much alike. Which of these catch phrases of the late 60s was used often in the song.....?

A power to the people
  B different strokes for different folks
  C what's happening?
  D it's a groovy situation   {79% correct on the Internet}

18. How about a Marvin Gaye hit from 1969? It was called TOO BUSY THINKING ABOUT MY BABY and it made it to No. 4. Throughout the song, Marvin tells us the result of what's going on in the title. He.....?
  A can't get a witness
  B ain't too proud to beg
  C ain't got time for nothing else
  D can't shake loose   {82% correct on the Internet}

19. We'll do one more from Sly & The Family Stone, again from 1969. It made it to No. 2 and was called HOT FUN IN THE SUMMERTIME. The only specific place mentioned was in the country.....where "everything is cool". It was the.....?
  A old red barn
  B ol' swimmin' hole
  C county fair
  D pool hall   {29% correct on the Internet}

20. Staying in 1969, with the first big hit for Tyrone Davis, who first recorded as "Tyrone The Wonder Boy". It was a very soulful tune called CAN I CHANGE MY MIND. What does Tyrone say his woman didn't do as he packed his bags to leave.....?
  A shed a tear
  B bat an eye
  C give a hoot
  D give two hoots   {28% correct on the Internet}

GAME 7 - TOUGH SOUL (60s/70s)

This is a tough game. It includes a question (#4) that was answered correctly on the Internet only 13% of the time. Good luck!

1. We are going to start this quiz with kind of a "feature" group....The Miracles. Their first charting song was also a big hit, called SHOP AROUND. In this 1961 song, they got the "better shop around" advice from Mom. What did she say about pretty girls.....?
   A they only break your heart
   B they come a dime a dozen
   C beauty's only skin deep, yeah, yeah, yeah
   D they wear too much makeup   {70% correct on the Internet}

2. In 1966, The Supremes topped the charts with YOU KEEP ME HANGIN' ON. It was a No. 1 on the Top 40 and R&B charts. Well, she wants him to get out of her life and to set her free. They can't be friends, because she says that when she sees him, it.....
   A makes her want to cry
   B makes she want to shout, "Hey, there!"
   C gives her the heebie-jeebies
   D only breaks her heart again   {85% correct on the Internet}

3. Also in 1966, Wilson Pickett had a smash with 634-5789 (SOULSVILLE, U.S.A.). This song was an R&B No. 1 for seven weeks! The Wicked Pickett tells the lady that if she picks up the telephone and dials the number, she won't have any more.....
   A night time blues
   B car problems
   C lonely nights
   D alien abductions   {70% correct on the Internet}

4. James Brown had one of his many hits in 1966 with IT'S A MAN'S MAN'S MAN'S WORLD, which spent two weeks at the top of the R&B charts. Right at the end of the song, James says that without a woman, a man is lost in two places, which are.....
   A in Brooklyn and Bayonne
   B in loneliness, and in sadness

C in the wilderness, and in bitterness
   D in absentia, and in vitro fertilization {13% correct on the Internet}

5. Let's get one from the mighty Temptations, also from 1966. That year BEAUTY IS ONLY SKIN DEEP was No.1 on the R&B charts for five weeks. When the singer's friends ask what he sees in his lady, he says she has what "ever-lovin' rare quality".....?
   A looks pretty in pink
   B she sure can cook, baby
   C sweet as can be
   D a pleasing personality   {29% correct on the Internet}

6. Back to the Miracles, with a song from 1963. That year, they made it into the top ten with MICKEY'S MONKEY. Written by Holland, Dozier and Holland, this song (lum dee lum dee lie, lum dee lum dee lie) is really all about what.....?
   A Mickey breaking the singer's heart
   B Mickey's new pet
   C Mickey's new Beanie Baby
   D Mickey's new dance   {67% correct on the Internet}

7. In 1967, Marvin Gaye and the late Tammi Terrell made it into the top ten with a song called YOUR PRECIOUS LOVE. In this nice love song, we are told where this precious love must have come from, which is.....
   A under the boardwalk
   B heaven must have sent it
   C over the rainbow, shiny and bright
   D from dreamland   {91% correct on the Internet}

8. Time for the Supremes. In 1967, they had another Top 40 and R&B No. 1 with LOVE IS HERE AND NOW YOU'RE GONE. The poor girls were having such a bad time....it seems that they fell in love, and instead of tenderness, they found.....
   A that it hurts so bad
   B heartache, instead
   C that guys are jerks
   D loneliness, loneliness   {70% correct on the Internet}

9. Funky time! In 1967, James Brown had another hit with COLD SWEAT - PART 1. This one was an R&B No. 1 for three weeks. It starts with James saying that he doesn't care about his lady's past, he says he just wants.....
   A their love to last
   B to say, "Avast!"
   C to have a blast
   D to move real fast   {77% correct on the Internet}

10. In 1969, The Dells hit the top ten with a remake of a 1956 hit called OH, WHAT A NIGHT (without an exclamation point). Guys are supposed to recall that special night, and their special girl. The singer says, with all the squeezin' and kissin', that's why.....
   A "we don't need any mistletoe"
   B "I love you so"
   C "I want our love to grow"
   D "you must be a pro"   {54% correct on the Internet}

11. More Diana Ross and The Supremes, this time from 1969 with SOMEDAY WE'LL BE TOGETHER. Once again, the song was No. 1 on the top 40 and R&B charts. The cause of the problem for Diana in this song is that she says she....?
   A didn't like baseball
   B made a big mistake and said goodbye
   C repeatedly stepped on his feet while dancing
   D ignored him once too often   {91% correct on the Internet}

12. Moving ahead a bit, into the early 70s, we have one of Stevie Wonder's biggest hits, called SUPERSTITION. Also No. 1 on the top 40 and R&B charts, it was one of Stevie's many hits. Complete the opening line - "Very superstitious.....
   A grab your coat and hat"
   B nip it in the bud"
   C you must be a fool"
   D writing's on the wall"   {90% correct on the Internet}

13. Not long after Superstition topped the charts, Stevie Wonder did it again with YOU ARE THE SUNSHINE OF MY LIFE, which hit No. 1 in the Spring of 1973. Stevie says that he feels that this is the beginning, though he has loved her for.....
  A ever
  B just five years
  C 42 years
  D a million years   {75% correct on the Internet}

14. In 1973, Marvin Gaye had one of his biggest hits with LET'S GET IT ON. This was just after his relevant period of songs like Inner City Blues and Mercy Mercy Me. At the beginning of this song, Marvin says that we are all.....
  A kind of goofy, but we need love anyway
  B lovers, with just one place to go
  C sensitive people, with so much to give
  D just friends, but wanting much more   {43% correct on the Internet}

15. It's another Miracles song, but now with Smokey Robinson designated as lead singer. In 1967, they had an R&B No.1 with I SECOND THAT EMOTION. Smokey doesn't want a one-night stand with this lady, and says that a taste of honey is.....
  A kind of sticky
  B like kisses, sweeter than wine
  C the cats, man
  D worse than none at all   {48% correct on the Internet}

16. In 1973, Eddie Kendricks, former lead singer of the Temptations, had a solo No.1 with KEEP ON TRUCKIN' (PART 1). This was another double No.1 (top 40 and R&B). Complete this line from Mr. Kendricks..."I've got a fever risin' with desire.....
  A if this keeps up, I just may retire"
  B I can't help myself and love burns like a pyre"
  C lets get together to see what may transpire"
  D it's my love jones and I feel like I'm on fire"   {34% correct on the Internet}

17. In 1973, Harold Melvin And The Blue Notes had a gold record with THE LOVE I LOST. Capturing "the sound of Philadelphia", lead singer Teddy Pendergrass tells us something went wrong, they just couldn't get along, and the love he lost was.....
  A a sweet love, and complete love
  B really hot, man, really hot
  C really cool, man, really cool
  D a love beyond compare   {47% correct on the Internet}

18. In 1977, singer and actress Thelma Houston hit the top with DON'T LEAVE ME THIS WAY. It was really her only hit, but a big one. At the end of the song, Thelma keeps telling her man not to leave her that way and to.....
  A satisfy the need in her
  B give her a cigarette
  C do, do, do his thing
  D get down tonight   {77% correct on the Internet}

19. The Commodores biggest hit was THREE TIMES A LADY, from 1978. It was a "triple No.1"...top 40, R&B and adult contemporary! We're not sure what it means (a kiss-off?), but at the beginning of the song where do they say they've come.....?
  A 148 Bonnie Meadow Road
  B under the boardwalk
  C to the end of their rainbow
  D to a river they can't cross   {68% correct on the Internet}

20. We will end with another one from Smokey Robinson & The Miracles. THE TEARS OF A CLOWN was a big 1970 hit. At the beginning of the song, Smokey tells his baby that if there is a smile on his clown-face, it's only there to.....
  A hide his cryin' eyes
  B fool the public
  C let the show go on
  D to be turned upside down   {59% correct on the Internet}

GAME 8 - QUICKIES FROM THE 60s AND 70s

You'll be done in no time, but you'll have a good time!

1. The day that can't be trusted, according to The Mamas & The Papas.
   A Friday
   B Saturday
   C Sunday
   D Monday   {87% correct on the Internet}

2. The day spent in the park, according to Chicago.
   A Friday
   B Saturday
   C Sunday
   D Monday   {88% correct on the Internet}

3. The day I have "on my mind," according to the Easybeats.
   A Friday
   B Saturday
   C Sunday
   D Monday   {70% correct on the Internet}

4. Which one makes my heart sing, and makes everything groovy?
   A This Diamond Ring by Gary Lewis and the Playboys
   B My Ding-A-Ling by Chuck Berry
   C Wild Thing by the Troggs
   D It's Your Thing by the Isley Brothers   {95% correct on the Internet}

5. This is shining and gleaming and streaming.
   A This Diamond Ring by Gary Lewis and the Playboys
   B Diamond Girl by Seals and Crofts
   C Little Star by the Elegants
   D Hair by the Cowsills
   E Sunny by Bobby Hebb   {75% correct on the Internet}

90

6. This can be found on a "clay and granite planet" in an age when "we're like tigers in a cage":
   A Africa by Toto
   B Mountain of Love by Harold Dorman
   C Sea of Love by Phil Phillips
   D Town Without Pity by Gene Pitney   {46% correct on the Internet}

7. In "Alone Again, Naturally," where did Gilbert O'Sullivan think about going to commit suicide?
   A tower
   B cliff
   C bedroom
   D graveyard
   E church   {30% correct on the Internet}

8. In Don McLean's "American Pie," a girl was seen dancing where?
   A On the beach
   B At the ball
   C In the gym
   D In a dream   {73% correct on the Internet}

9. This person's "war machines" are not needed:
   A Mr. Custer by Larry Verne
   B Soldier Boy by the Shirelles
   C Island Girl by Elton John
   D American Woman by the Guess Who
   E Lady Madonna by the Beatles   {73% correct on the Internet}

10. Who turned out to be a "crazy" person?
    A Angie Baby by Helen Reddy
    B Billie Jean by Michael Jackson
    C Brandy by Looking Glass
    D Cracklin' Rosie by Neil Diamond
    E Honey by Bobby Goldsboro   {61% correct on the Internet}

11. The Doobies' "Black Water" refers to which river?
   A Mississippi River
   B Savannah River
   C River Jordan
   D Charles River
   E Joan Rivers   {82% correct on the Internet}

12. The Standells' "Dirty Water" can be found in this city:
   A Detroit
   B Boston
   C Atlanta
   D New Orleans   {44% correct on the Internet}

13. Which one was chosen after it was determined that Betty Lou and Peggy Sue wouldn't do?
   A Marianne by the Hilltoppers
   B Carrie Ann by the Hollies
   C Barbara Ann by the Beach Boys
   D Anna by the Beatles
   E Ramona by Ernest T. Bass   {79% correct on the Internet}

14. Name the vehicle that had "3 deuces and a 4-speed and a 389"?
   A GTO by Ronny and the Daytonas
   B 409 by the Beach Boys
   C Little Deuce Coupe by the Beach Boys
   D Hod Rod Lincoln by Commander Cody
   E Chevy Van by Sammy Johns   {50% correct on the Internet}

15. In which of these songs was champagne preferred over health food?
   A Brandy by Looking Glass
   B Margaritaville by Jimmy Buffett
   C Escape (the pina colada song) by Rupert Holmes
   D Bottle of Wine by the Fireballs
   E Spill the Wine by Eric Burdon and War   {62% correct on the Internet}

16. The singer excuses himself to kiss the sky in this song:
   A Fly Robin Fly by Silver Convention

B I Want to Take You Higher by Sly and the Family Stone
   C Purple Haze by Jimi Hendrix
   D Get off of my Cloud by the Rolling Stones   {89% correct on the Internet}

17. Who swings down the street in a "fancy-free" manner -- "window shopping, but never stopping to buy"?
   A Gloria by the Shadows of Knight
   B Gloria by Laura Branigan
   C Girl from Ipanema by Stan Getz and Astrud Gilberto
   D Georgie Girl by the Seekers
   E Gypsy Woman by Brian Hyland   {75% correct on the Internet}

18. Who "swings so smooth and sways so gently," and when she goes by everyone says 'aahhh'?
   A Gloria by the Shadows of Knight
   B Gloria by Laura Branigan
   C Girl from Ipanema by Stan Getz and Astrud Gilberto
   D Georgie Girl by the Seekers
   E Gypsy Woman by Brian Hyland   {68% correct on the Internet}

19. Who was "about 5-feet 4 from her head to the ground"?
   A Gloria by the Shadows of Knight
   B Gloria by Laura Branigan
   C Girl from Ipanema by Stan Getz and Astrud Gilberto
   D Georgie Girl by the Seekers
   E Gypsy Woman by Brian Hyland   {53% correct on the Internet}

20. Our final ten-cents worth......which song does NOT mention the word "dime" (the other songs say "have you got a dime?...you can keep the dime...save up every dime...one thin dime won't even shine your shoes"):
   A I'm Down by the Beatles
   B Operator by Jim Croce
   C Bad Girls by Donna Summer
   D On Broadway by the Drifters
   E Down in the Boondocks by Billie Joe Royal   {49% correct on the Internet}

GAME 9 - WHO-WHAT-WHERE IN THE 60s AND 70s

People, places, and things from some notable songs...

1. The Beatles' Jojo left this city. Get back, Jojo.
   A Seattle
   B San Francisco
   C Tucson
   D Houston
   E Liverpool   {84% correct on the Internet}

2. Had silver hair and baggy pants, and jumped so high.
   A Dancing Queen by Abba
   B Mr. Bojangles by the Nitty Gritty Dirt Band
   C Shannon by Henry Gross
   D Jet by Paul McCartney
   E Jumpin' Jack Flash by the Rolling Stones   {80% correct on the Internet}

3. Our first "line dancing" question: which song came first? (It was the only 60's song -- the rest were in the 70's.)
   A Hold The Line by Toto
   B Dragging The Line by Tommy James
   C Right Down The Line by Gerry Rafferty
   D I Got A Line On You by Spirit
   E One Toke Over The Line by Brewer & Shipley   {24% correct on the Internet}

4. Part of Blue Swede's being "Hooked On A Feeling."
   A come-a come-a come-a
   B rama lama ding-dong
   C dingy-dong ding
   D ooga chucka ooga-ooga   {80% correct on the Internet}

5. America was going there to find Daisy Jane.
   A Kansas City
   B Memphis
   C New Orleans
   D Boston   {51% correct on the Internet}

6. I've got a crush on you, with your eyes so blue, doo-bee-doo:
   A Diana by Paul Anka
   B Denise by Randy and the Rainbows
   C Donna by Ritchie Valens
   D Domino by Van Morrison
   E Dominique by the Singing Nun   {46% correct on the Internet}

7. Has big, brown eyes. And it's "goodbye heart" when you say hello to her.
   A Mary Lou
   B Peggy Sue
   C Suzy Q
   D Billie Joe
   E Blue Eyes   {76% correct on the Internet}

8. This is "sure to shine."
   A Sunny by Bobbie Hebb
   B Sunshine Superman by Donovan
   C Sunshine On My Shoulders by John Denver
   D Diamond Girl by Seals & Crofts
   E Dirty Water by the Standells   {69% correct on the Internet}

9. The worst person I know.
   A Leroy Brown by Jim Croce
   B Mother-In-Law by Ernie K-Doe
   C Maneater by Daryl Hall & John Oates
   D Witchy Woman by the Eagles   {67% correct on the Internet}

10. Which one will be haunted like a ghost till she's "mine"?
    A Ruby Baby by Dion
    B Ruby Tuesday by the Rolling Stones
    C Black Magic Woman by Santana
    D Dream Weaver by Gary Wright
    E Spooky by the Classics IV   {26% correct on the Internet}

11. The one that did NOT, as far as we know, go away.
   A Go Away Little Girl by Steve Lawrence
   B Walk Away, Renee by Left Banke
   C Pretty Woman by Roy Orbison
   D Mandy by Barry Manilow
   E Runaway by Del Shannon   {57% correct on the Internet}

12. Elton John's Rocket Man thinks this is not the place to raise your kids.
   A Mercury
   B Venus
   C Earth
   D Mars
   E Suburbia   {57% correct on the Internet}

13. Was the ruin of many young boys down New Orleans way.
   A Black Magic Woman by Santana
   B Honky Tonk Woman by the Rolling Stones
   C Witchy Woman by the Eagles
   D Hotel California by the Eagles
   E House of the Rising Sun by the Animals   {84% correct on the Internet}

14. When you're feeling tired and beat, the air is fresh and sweet there.
   A My Little Town by Simon & Garfunkle
   B McArthur Park by Richard Harris
   C Mountain of Love by Harold Dorman
   D Up on the Roof by the Drifters
   E Down in the Boondocks by Billie Joe Royal   {71% correct on the Internet}

15. Otis Redding was sitting on the "Dock of the Bay," but according to the song what state was he from?
   A Louisiana
   B Texas
   C Georgia
   D Colorado
   E California   {63% correct on the Internet}

16. The one that leads the singer to a door.
   A Country Roads by John Denver
   B Long and Winding Road by the Beatles
   C Carefree Highway by Gordon Lightfoot
   D Long Lonesome Highway by Michael Parks   {83% correct on the Internet}

17. The one that goes to the mountains and the plains.
   A Country Roads by John Denver
   B Long and Winding Road by the Beatles
   C Carefree Highway by Gordon Lightfoot
   D Long Lonesome Highway by Michael Parks   {36% correct on the Internet}

18. The one that takes the singer home to "mountain mama."
   A Country Roads by John Denver
   B Long and Winding Road by the Beatles
   C Carefree Highway by Gordon Lightfoot
   D Long Lonesome Highway by Michael Parks   {88% correct on the Internet}

19. Who or what can we find in the baddest part of Chicago?
   A Sugar Shack by Jimmy Gilmer & the Fireballs
   B Mountain of Love by Harold Dorman
   C Sir Duke by Stevie Wonder
   D Big Bad John by Jimmy Dean
   E Bad Bad Leroy Brown by Jim Croce   {82% correct on the Internet}

20. Which one am I "stuck like glue" to?
   A My Girl by the Temptations
   B My Guy by Mary Wells
   C My Sweet Lord by George Harrison
   D My Cherie Amour by Stevie Wonder
   E Stupid Cupid by Connie Francis   {79% correct on the Internet}

GAME 10 - MORE QUICKIES FROM THE 60s AND 70s

Ready for more? Some toughies here. Only 9% of our Internet players originally got Question 2 right, so we added a hint.

1. He/She/They proclaimed: "Different strokes for different folks!"
   A Stevie Wonder
   B Sly and the Family Stone
   C Aretha Franklin
   D The Temptations
   E John Denver   {79% correct on the Internet}

2. Starts up north at Hollywood. (Not the city of, but a street in Chicago....when it first came out, the DJs edited out the "drug" reference.)
   A Baker Street
   B Little Old Lady from Pasadena
   C Ventura Highway
   D Lake Shore Drive   {9% correct on the Internet (before the hint about Chicago)}

3. The one sung by a woman. She doesn't really have it so bad, tho.
   A 8 Days a Week
   B 9 to 5
   C 25 or 6 to 4
   D 50 Ways to Leave Your Lover
   E 96 Tears   {92% correct on the Internet}

4. Recommended by Mr. M.D. Yeah, yeah.
   A Good Lovin'
   B Respect
   C Sugar, Sugar
   D Sweet Soul Music
   E Love Potion No. 9   {63% correct on the Internet}

5. Gives you "excitations." No, this wasn't done by Rhymin' Simon.
   A Sweet Soul Music
   B Hot Fun in the Summertime

C Hanky Panky
   D Wild Thing
   E Good Vibrations   {93% correct on the Internet}

6. According to Petula, this is where we can forget all our troubles and cares:
   A At the Hop
   B Kokomo
   C Surf City
   D Downtown
   E Hotel California   {85% correct on the Internet}

7. The Beach Boys said this part of the U.S. had good kissers. Cuddle up, kids.
   A North
   B South
   C East
   D Midwest
   E California   {55% correct on the Internet}

8. In "Fun, Fun, Fun" daddy thought his daughter was going here.
   A Store
   B Church
   C School
   D Library
   E Lube Express   {73% correct on the Internet}

9. Which of these places was NOT the site of a "midnight" song. Someone walked there, tho.
   A Oasis
   B Train
   C Moscow
   D Memphis   {61% correct on the Internet}

10. The one that DID NOT sing "How Sweet It Is (To Be Loved By You)." Seems like his kind of song, though.
   A Marvin Gaye
   B John Denver

   C James Taylor
   D Junior Walker   {56% correct on the Internet}

11. Which one DID NOT sing "Hurt So Bad"? Seems NOT like his/her/their kind of song.
   A Little Anthony
   B Lettermen
   C Linda Ronstadt
   D Led Zeppelin   {66% correct on the Internet}

12. The song that was set in the early fall (back-to-school time).
   A Maggie May
   B Saturday in the Park
   C Oh, What a Night
   D Ode to Billie Joe   {66% correct on the Internet}

13. The singer(s) of this song had a name with a fruit in it. Set the alarm clock and think for awhile.
   A Crimson and Clover
   B Apple, Peaches, Pumpkin Pie
   C Sugar and Spice
   D Peppermint Twist
   E Incense and Peppermints   {59% correct on the Internet}

14. One of these is not really referring to a location. It's referring to a mode of transportation! Which one?
   A Sweet Home Chicago
   B Sweet Home Alabama
   C City of New Orleans
   D Town Without Pity   {36% correct on the Internet}

15. As song titles go, there's no California _____. (But there's a USA variety)
   A Dreamin'
   B Girls
   C Sun
   D Surfin'   {57% correct on the Internet}

16. Mental state caused by meeting your old lover in the street. Might make you drink some beers.
   A Love Hangover
   B Dizzy
   C Mind Games
   D Still Crazy After All These Years
   E Kind of a Drag   {41% correct on the Internet}

17. A sudden rage, the next phase. It had "appeal", anyway.
   A Mellow Yellow
   B Green Tambourine
   C Brown Sugar
   D Deep Purple   {59% correct on the Internet}

18. Turns my mind into stone.
   A Deep Purple
   B Blue Moon
   C White Room
   D Black Magic Woman   {60% correct on the Internet}

19. Hey! School's over, so we can get married. Talk about a perfect match.
   A Hey Joe
   B Hey Jude
   C Hey Paula
   D Hey Girl
   E Hey Baby   {66% correct on the Internet}

20. The singer of this song lived on spongecake and was bitter. And sweet and sour and salty.
   A Sugar Town
   B Candy Man
   C Margaritaville
   D Sugar, Sugar
   E The Pina Colada Song   {80% correct on the Internet}

Chapter 3 - The 70s

GAME 1 - SLIPPIN' THROUGH THE 70s

This game has some of the most popular 70s songs in it....lots of chances to show you know your music trivia!

1. This was originally the B-side of Rod Stewart's Reason to Believe. Here we go with lots of clues -- late September, she stole his heart, wrecked his bed, made a fool of him, and, in the morning sun, she looked quite old. She's.....
  A Layla
  B Maggie May
  C Judy In Disguise (With Glasses)
  D Ruby Tuesday   {96% correct on the Internet}

2. Somewhat psychedelically (yes, that's a word), Norman Greenbaum tells us that he wants to go somewhere when he dies. He even goes so far as to proselytize (another real word). If he makes it to this place, he will see.....
  A Earth Angel
  B My Sweet Lord
  C Spirit In The Sky
  D Long Cool Woman (In A Black Dress)   {92% correct on the Internet}

3. Breakin' up may be hard to do, but it seems to happen all the time, even in the 70s. Now, Tyrone Davis wants to go home, and leavin' would be the last thing on his mind, if he could just do this.....
  A Turn Back The Hands Of Time
  B Love Her Madly
  C Knock Three Times
  D Get Back   {91% correct on the Internet}

4. "Here comes the big boss.....!" Everybody was doing this, even Funky Billy Chin. Does this song deserve to be a candidate for the worst song of the 70s? You decide. It did make #1 in the U.S. and U.K., and that must have made Karl Douglas happy.....
  A The Hustle
  B Ballroom Blitz

C Working In The Coal Mine
   D Kung Fu Fighting   {77% correct on the Internet}

5. Was it a fantasy? Did this really happen to Sammy Johns or not? He was on the road and he meets this beautiful young woman, and almost just like that.....! He actually told her to "get some sleep and dream of rock and roll" in.....
   A My Little Town
   B Sweet Home Alabama
   C Chevy Van
   D Hotel California   {76% correct on the Internet}

6. Vanity Fair's lead singer is almost drowning in the pouring rain. He has to get back to his baby. Hurry, hurry, she must be awfully impatient. So, to get back, he's.....
   A Jumpin' Jack Flash
   B Hitchin' A Ride
   C Draggin' The Line
   D Twistin' The Night Away {86% correct on the Internet}

7. Michael Murphey went on to become a country star, but he sang this song about a woman who died during a "killin' frost", looking for her pony (I guess). Now she's looking for Michael. The pony's name.....
   A Shannon
   B Secretariat
   C Wildfire
   D A Horse With No Name   {84% correct on the Internet}

8. The most depressing song of the 70s? Perhaps, but this 10cc song was #1 in the U.K. and peaked at #2 in the U.S. Remember her picture on the wall, hiding the nasty stain? He just won't commit, and he says.....
   A I'm Not In Love
   B Love Hurts
   C All Out Of Love
   D Love Is Blue   {66% correct on the Internet}

9. Many listeners must have thought that the event in this song occurred a long time ago. In fact, it was in 1975. Gordon Lightfoot told about what the treacherous waters of Lake Superior can do in.....
  A Ride, Captain, Ride
  B Proud Mary
  C Cold As Ice
  D The Wreck Of The Edmund Fitzgerald   {81% correct on the Internet}

10. The Nitty Gritty Dirt Band told us about this odd fellow. He had silver hair, jumped so high (we don't know why), clicked his heels and apparently spent a lot of time in jails. Of course, it's.....
  A Old Rivers
  B Mr. Wendal
  C Mr. Bojangles
  D Jumpin' Jack Flash   {89% correct on the Internet}

11. There's this song by Derek and the Dominoes which never seems to end. Eric Clapton slowed it down even more and had a bigger hit. Anyway, the subject of this song has someone madly in love with her. She's.....
  A Layla
  B Lola
  C Judy In Disguise (With Glasses)
  D Ruby Tuesday   {95% correct on the Internet}

12. Jim Croce sang of this "bad dude" from the southside of Chicago. He was apparently based on someone Croce met while at Fort Dix, New Jersey. He was meaner than a junkyard dog, and known as.....
  A Big, Bad John
  B Mr. Bojangles
  C Bad, Bad Leroy Brown
  D Superfly   {94% correct on the Internet}

13. Hmmm.....she's heading to the cheatin' side of town.....where's that? The Eagles lift our spirits (not!) with this song about a woman married to a cold, old guy and has a young stud on the side. She's got.....

A Hungry Eyes
B Bette Davis Eyes
C Lyin' Eyes
D Private Eyes   {90% correct on the Internet}

14. How about a nice love song? It was one of six million-sellers for the Stylistics. It also has two lead vocalists (listen carefully next time you hear it). Anyway, she taught him how to live again, it's.....
  A The Way We Were
  B I'll Have To Say I Love You In A Song
  C Thank God I'm A Country Boy
  D You Make Me Feel Brand New   {83% correct on the Internet}

15. Bounce around! The Spinners said he's guaranteed to blow your mind (that happened a lot in the 70s). This fella' makes a unique sound by playing a unique "instrument". So, prepare yourself for.....
  A The Entertainer
  B Jazzman
  C Disco Duck
  D Rubberband Man   {91% correct on the Internet}

16. James Taylor made just about everyone feel good with this song. The message is quite clear that the singee(?) should never worry about life's trials and tribulations, because with James.....
  A You Don't Have To Be A Star
  B Love Will Keep Us Together
  C (Shake, Shake, Shake) Shake Your Booty
  D You've Got A Friend   {93% correct on the Internet}

17. Guess you could call this the "ooga-chukka song". Blue Swede seems to have done better than B. J. Thomas with their unique remake. But, neither performer needs a cure for this bug, from a nameless girl. It's.....
  A Hooked On A Feeling
  B Feelings
  C Feels Like The First Time
  D Crocodile Rock   {92% correct on the Internet}

18. This song was supposed to be about witches, or something supernatural. King Harvest told this story of a happy group of people having some kind of fun after darkness falls.....
   A Night Fever
   B Dancing In The Moonlight
   C Boogaloo Down Broadway
   D Monster Mash   {65% correct on the Internet}

19. She's got it, yeah, baby, she's got it.....this time, the original by Shocking Blue beats out the popular remake by Bananarama. And, Frankie Avalon sang a different tune about.....
   A Venus
   B Honey
   C Short, Fat Fanny
   D Sherry   {97% correct on the Internet}

20. Wait a minute.....it's the 70s.....we can't leave without.....a DISCO song! (Keep your opinions on this to yourself, please.) Alicia Bridges wanted to go out and boogie (didn't everyone?). She wanted "ack-shun". She said.....
   A Never Can Say Goodbye
   B Disco Duck
   C I Love The Nightlife (Disco 'Round)
   D Play That Funky Music   {90% correct on the Internet}

GAME 2 - WHO SANG THESE? (70s)

Once again.....pick the correct artist....top ten songs in caps. With some of these performers, we can fool hardly anyone.

1. IF YOU LEAVE ME NOW; BABY, WHAT A BIG SURPRISE; CALL ON ME; SATURDAY IN THE PARK; Wishing You Were Here; Free.....
   A Bee Gees
   B Chicago
   C Wings
   D Fendermen
   E Air Supply   {94% correct on the Internet}

2. RIKKI, DON'T LOSE THAT NUMBER; DO IT AGAIN; Reeling In The Years; Peg; Josie; Black Friday.....
   A Steam
   B Blues Magoos
   C REO Speedwagon
   D Blondie
   E Steely Dan   {90% correct on the Internet}

3. ONE LESS BELL TO ANSWER; (LAST NIGHT) I DIDN'T GET TO SLEEP AT ALL; IF I COULD REACH YOU; Never My Love; Puppet Man; Save The Country.....
   A The Fifth Estate
   B The Supremes
   C The Three Degrees
   D The 5th Dimension
   E The Miracles   {73% correct on the Internet}

4. SWEET LOVE; JUST TO BE CLOSE TO YOU; BRICK HOUSE; SAIL ON; Too Hot Ta Trot; Slippery When Wet.....
   A The Crazy World Of Arthur Brown
   B Earth, Wind & Fire
   C Commodores
   D Gladys Knight & The Pips
   E Kool & The Gang   {68% correct on the Internet}

5. WITCHY WOMAN; ONE OF THESE NIGHTS; LYIN' EYES; BEST OF MY LOVE; Already Gone; Peaceful Easy Feeling.....
   A America
   B The Little Dippers
   C Three Dog Night
   D Culture Club
   E Eagles   {92% correct on the Internet}

6. BABY I'M-A WANT YOU; MAKE IT WITH YOU; IT DON'T MATTER TO ME; IF; Let Your Love Go; Diary.....
   A ABBA
   B Moody Blues
   C Monkees
   D Bread
   E Love Unlimited Orchestra   {87% correct on the Internet}

7. FEELS LIKE THE FIRST TIME; HOT BLOODED; DOUBLE VISION; COLD AS ICE; Head Games; Dirty White Boy.....
   A Fleetwood Mac
   B Foreigner
   C Grand Funk
   D Boston
   E Pink Floyd   {93% correct on the Internet}

8. LADY; COME SAIL AWAY; BABE; Lorelei; Blue Collar Man (Long Nights); Renegade.....
   A The Floaters
   B Stylistics
   C Styx
   D Little River Band
   E Steve Miller Band   {84% correct on the Internet}

9. LONG TRAIN RUNNIN'; BLACK WATER; WHAT A FOOL BELIEVES; Minute By Minute; Takin' It To The Streets; China Grove.....
   A Doobie Brothers
   B Lynyrd Skynyrd
   C Stampeders

D Bachman Turner Overdrive
   E Grand Funk   {93% correct on the Internet}

10. ONE BAD APPLE; YO-YO; DOWN BY THE LAZY RIVER; LOVE ME FOR A REASON; Hold Her Tight; Crazy Horses.....
   A Hues Corporation
   B The Osmonds
   C Tony Orlando & Dawn
   D Partridge Family
   E Jackson Five   {61% correct on the Internet}

11. Some solo performers now. Starting with SONG SUNG BLUE; LONGFELLOW SERENADE; I AM...I SAID; Play Me; If You Know What I Mean; Desiree.....
   A Barry Manilow
   B Freddy Fender
   C Neil Sedaka
   D B.J. Thomas
   E Neil Diamond   {88% correct on the Internet}

12. RHINESTONE COWBOY; SOUTHERN NIGHTS; IT'S ONLY MAKE BELIEVE; Honey Come Back; Country Boy (You Got Your Feet In L.A.); Sunflower.....
   A Pepino The Italian Mouse
   B Ray Stevens
   C John Denver
   D Glen Campbell
   E Mac Davis   {87% correct on the Internet}

13. GYPSYS, TRAMPS & THIEVES; YOU BETTER SIT DOWN KIDS; HALF-BREED; DARK LADY; THE WAY OF LOVE; Living In A House Divided.....
   A Cher
   B Debby Boone
   C Barbra Streisand
   D Vicki Lawrence
   E Bette Midler   {86% correct on the Internet}

14. SUPERSTITION; LIVING FOR THE CITY; HIGHER GROUND; SIR DUKE; BOOGIE ON REGGAE WOMAN; I WISH.....
   A Stevie Wonder
   B Donny Osmond
   C Elton John
   D Marvin Gaye
   E Billy Preston   {90% correct on the Internet}

15. PHOTOGRAPH; YOU'RE SIXTEEN; ONLY YOU; OH MY MY; BACK OFF BOOGALOO; IT DON'T COME EASY.....
   A Fantastic Johnny C
   B Paul Simon
   C Al Green
   D George Harrison
   E Ringo Starr   {71% correct on the Internet}

16. YOU'RE NO GOOD; WHEN WILL I BE LOVED; BLUE BAYOU; IT'S SO EASY; Tracks Of My Tears; That'll Be The Day.....
   A Diana Ross
   B Helen Reddy
   C Linda Ronstadt
   D Little Peggy March
   E Aretha Franklin   {89% correct on the Internet}

17. THE WONDER OF YOU; BURNING LOVE; You Don't Have To Say You Love Me; Kentucky Rain; Promised Land; My Boy.....
   A Wilson Pickett
   B John Travolta
   C B.J. Thomas
   D Elvis Presley
   E John Denver   {73% correct on the Internet}

18. IT'S TOO LATE; SWEET SEASONS; JAZZMAN; NIGHTINGALE; So Far Away; Only Love Is Real.....
   A The Singing Nun
   B Carole King
   C Roberta Flack

D Donna Summer
   E Carly Simon   {75% correct on the Internet}

19. JUST THE WAY YOU ARE; MY LIFE; Piano Man; Only The Good Die Young; She's Always A Woman; Big Shot.....
   A Elton John
   B Nervous Norvus
   C Billy Joel
   D Jim Croce
   E Paul Simon   {95% correct on the Internet}

20. DON'T EXPECT ME TO BE YOUR FRIEND; ME AND YOU AND A DOG NAMED BOO; It Sure Took A Long, Long Time; How Can I Tell Her; Don't Tell Me Goodnight; Where Were You When I Was Falling In Love.....
   A Joe South
   B Nilsson
   C Lobo
   D Kenny Loggins
   E Gilbert O'Sullivan {68% correct on the Internet}

GAME 3 - FLASHBACKS FROM THE 70s

Simple clues, simple answers.......well, many of them, anyway.

1. Someone was "Sittin' downtown in a railway station", waiting for a train home. We all hope that the train was on time. The song title gives us a hint about the state of mind of the singer(s):
   A Anticipation by Carly Simon
   B Draggin' The Line by Tommy James
   C Hooked On A Feeling by Blue Swede
   D Love Train by the O'Jays
   E One Toke Over The Line by Brewer and Shipley   {63% correct on the Internet}

2. This song considers the possibility of no heaven, no hell, no religion, and everyone living in peace!
   A Dust In The Wind by Kansas
   B Golden Years by David Bowie
   C Imagine by John Lennon
   D Morning Has Broken by Cat Stevens
   E What A Fool Believes by the Doobie Brothers   {95% correct on the Internet}

3. The singer's brother is "traveling tonight on a plane." The singer sees red taillights...and his brother waving goodbye...
   A Brother Louie by Stories
   B Daniel by Elton John
   C Fernando by Abba
   D Poetry Man by Phoebe Snow
   E Vincent by Don McLean   {87% correct on the Internet}

4. The "Jailer Man and Sailor Sam" were searching for this:
   A Band On The Run by Paul McCartney
   B Brandy by Looking Glass
   C Gold by John Stewart
   D Seasons In The Sun by Terry Jacks
   E Sweet Thing by Rufus featuring Chaka Khan   {75% correct on the Internet}

5. This song told the story about a father who never had time for his little boy, and then found out that his grown-up son didn't have time for him!
   A Lonely Boy by Donny Osmond
   B Cat's In The Cradle by Harry Chapin
   C Ships by Barry Manilow
   D Sundown by Gordon Lightfoot   {92% correct on the Internet}

6. This song expressed the singer's disdain for health food and yoga, and a
preference for champagne and making love at midnight:
   A American Pie by Don McLean
   B Escape by Rupert Holmes
   C That's The Way I Like It by KC and the Sunshine Band
   D How Sweet It Is by James Taylor   {77% correct on the Internet}

7. It was during the gales of November:
   A I Shot the Sheriff by Eric Clapton
   B Riders on the Storm by the Doors
   C War by Edwin Starr
   D Woodstock by Crosby, Stills, Nash, and Young
   E Wreck of the Edmund Fitzgerald by Gordon Lightfoot {76% correct on the Internet}

8. In "Goodbye Yellow Brick Road," Elton John sings about:
   A Dying
   B His visit to a land similar to Oz
   C Giving up the penthouse and returning to the farm
   D Another singer's plagiaristic use of an Elton John song {64% correct on the Internet}

9. Who asks you to hand him his walking cane and hat -- in a hurry, because he ain't got time to chat, and because he's "gotta move, gotta groove":
   A Rubberband Man by the Spinners
   B Sir Duke by Stevie Wonder
   C Music Box Dancer by Frank Mills

D Mr. Bojangles by the Nitty Gritty Dirt Band
   E Dancing Machine by the Jackson 5   {50% correct on the Internet}

10. What Diana Ross called the doctor for:
   A Double Vision
   B Night Fever
   C Boogie Fever
   D Sad Eyes
   E Love Hangover   {75% correct on the Internet}

11. Ahh, memories. She slapped Johnnie's face, and we all fell about the place laughing. But now the singer says:
   A The Bitch Is Back by Elton John
   B The Boys Are Back in Town by Thin Lizzy
   C I Want You Back by the Jackson 5
   D Baby Come Back by Player
   E (It's) Too Late to Turn Back Now by the Cornelius Brothers and Sister Rose   {68% correct on the Internet}

12. She's going out for the evening to give comfort an old friend. But, as we learn in this song, she's really heading for the "cheatin' side of town":
   A Sad Eyes by Robert John
   B Lyin' Eyes by the Eagles
   C Lucille by Kenny Rogers
   D Lonesome Loser by the Little River Band
   E If You Leave Me Now by Chicago   {85% correct on the Internet}

13. Do you think you are a superstar? Everyone shines, like the moon and the stars and the sun. This is what's going to get you!
   A Hot Stuff by Donna Summer
   B Bad Blood by Neil Sedaka
   C Lowdown by Boz Scaggs
   D Scorpio by Dennis Coffey
   E Instant Karma by John Ono Lennon {69% correct on the Internet}

14. The singer questions God's existence -- for if God really does exits, why would he desert anyone...?
   A Indiana Wants Me by R. Dean Taylor
   B Alone Again (Naturally) by Gilbert O'Sullivan
   C I Shot the Sheriff by Eric Clapton
   D One Toke Over the Line by Brewer and Shipley
   E Renegade by Styx   {79% correct on the Internet}

15. Lynyrd Skynyrd addresses a popular singer in "Sweet Home Alabama" to inform him about the merits of their fair state. Who was this singer?
   A Mick Jagger
   B Eric Clapton
   C Neil Young
   D Jackson Browne
   E Kenny Rogers   {77% correct on the Internet}

16. This was a 1970 "spiritual" hit that got the singer into a copyright hassle.
   A Angel Of The Morning by Merrilee Rush and the Turnabouts
   B Spirit In The Sky by Norman Greenbaum
   C My Sweet Lord by George Harrison
   D Signs by the Five Man Electrical Band   {87% correct on the Internet}

17. You're leavin' -- you can "take my heart, my soul, my money, but don't leave me here drowning in my tears"...
   A Don't Leave Me This Way by Thelma Houston
   B Don't Pull Your Love by Hamilton, Joe Frank, and Reynolds
   C I Just Wanna Stop by Gino Vanelli
   D Leaving On A Jet Plane by Peter Paul and Mary
   E Let's Stay Together by Al Green   {64% correct on the Internet}

18. In this song, the singer tells us that apparently only beauty queens find love, and that less-desirable girls resort to "inventing lovers on the phone."
   A At Seventeen by Janis Ian
   B Help Me by Joni Mitchell

C It's A Heartache by Bonnie Tyler
   D Lonely Night (Angel Face) by the Captain and Tennille
   E Lonely People by America {64% correct on the Internet}

19. It's "the word: it's got groove, it's got feeling..."
   A Emotion by Samantha Sang
   B Grease by Frankie Valli
   C Fire by the Ohio Players
   D Wildfire by Michael Murphey
   E Grease Fire by Huey Motid {79% correct on the Internet}

20. Who was broke in Baton Rouge, hitched a ride to New Orleans, and then sang songs with the "windshield wipers slappin' time..."?
   A Brother Louie by Stories
   B The Guitar Man by Bread
   C Just You 'N' Me by Chicago
   D Me And Bobby McGee by Janis Joplin
   E Ramblin' Man by the Allman Brothers Band {80% correct on the Internet}

GAME 4 - SLIDIN' THROUGH THE 70s

There are a couple of real toughies in this game, but, with a little skill and lots of concentration, you should do alright.

1. Starting in 1970, we'll begin with The Hollies and their mellow HE AIN'T HEAVY, HE'S MY BROTHER. If we ever do a quiz on songs with fancy-shmancy words, remember this one. They sing of the brother, he "will not _____me"......
   A disquiet
   B inarculate
   C encumber
   D bedraggle   {81% correct on the Internet}

2. Also in 1970, Van Morrison mumbled through a song called DOMINO, which made it to No. 3, but it's not easy to figure out what he is singing about. So, the question is not about the unintelligible Domino, but what classic "girl" hit Morrison also wrote....
   A Gloria (The Shadows of Night)
   B Alice Kramden (Nervous Norvus)
   C Maggie May (Rod Stewart)
   D Patches (Dickie Lee)   {69% correct on the Internet}

3. Moving on to 1971, Bill Withers had a gold single with a song called AIN'T NO SUNSHINE. In the middle of the song, and before he runs out of breath, Bill repeats a phrase a grand total of 26 times (we think we counted right). What is the phrase.......
   A beep, beep
   B I know
   C get back
   D it's true   {87% correct on the Internet}

4. One more from 1971, this time from Sly & The Family Stone. FAMILY AFFAIR was No.1 for three weeks (five weeks on the R&B charts). So, one child grows up to be somebody that just loves to learn, and another grows up to be.....
   A one that will just cause concern
   B somebody that says, "How's your fern?"

C one that will leave and never return
   D somebody you just love to burn   {33% correct on the Internet}

5. In the early 70s, Al Green had a string of seven consecutive gold singles! In 1972, LET'S STAY TOGETHER was an R&B No. 1 for nine weeks! The Stylistics might agree with Al's comment near the beginning of the song that she makes him feel so.....
   A full of soul
   B betcha, by golly, wow
   C like, special, man
   D brand new   {78% correct on the Internet}

6. More soul from 1972 with The O'Jays and BACK STABBERS, the first in their series of "relevant" records in the early 70s. It starts with a 39 second instrumental introduction and then we get hit with the musical question.....
   A "Hey, does that hurt, or what?"
   B "Can't you see?"
   C "What they doin'?"
   D "What's it all about, Alfie?"   {65% correct on the Internet}

7. On to 1973. This was the year that the group War had a gold record with a song called THE CISCO KID. According to the song, The Kid drank whiskey and Pancho drank the wine. And, where, according to the song, did they meet.....?
   A Blueberry Hill
   B on the border, Rio Grande
   C la cocina, every day
   D in the barroom, night and day   {64% correct on the Internet}

8. Also in 1973, Stealers Wheel did a song called STUCK IN THE MIDDLE WITH YOU, which is listed as the No. 50 song of the year. Led by Gerry Rafferty, they tell us that they are stuck in the middle, with clowns to the left, and whom, to the right.....?
   A jokers
   B commies
   C fakers
   D lunkheads   {95% correct on the Internet}

9. 1974 already! My, how time flies! Al Wilson made it to No. 1 that year with the soulful SHOW AND TELL. According to the song, which of the following is the best description of what "show and tell" is.....?
   A just for me and you, when we're all alone
   B just show me now, I promise not to tell
   C just a game he plays when he wants to say I love you
   D just a lie, when you told me goodbye   {61% correct on the Internet}

10. Also from 1974, The Hues Corporation had their only big hit with ROCK THE BOAT, which also made it to No.1. (Rock on with your bad self!) They say that their love is like a ship on the ocean and they've been sailing with a cargo full of.....
   A love's magic potion
   B hand and body lotion
   C my loving notion
   D love and devotion   {91% correct on the Internet}

11. We are now in 1975 and we should include an Elton John song. He did have 16 top ten songs in the 70s! The impressive list included PHILADELPHIA FREEDOM. This song was a tribute to a tennis team and which tennis star.....?
   A Billie Jean King
   B Bronco Nagurski
   C Chris Evert
   D Big Bill Tilden   {89% correct on the Internet}

12. The second song from the year 1975 is from one-hit wonder Ace, called HOW LONG. Lead singer Paul Carrack also sang lead on other hits, including The Living Years by Mike + The Mechanics. Anyway, complete the title line, how long.....
   A has this been going on
   B will you leave me this way
   C is a meter, anyway
   D can we sing this song   {93% correct on the Internet}

13. In 1976, Orleans had a top ten hit with STILL THE ONE, which ended up as a theme song for the ABC TV network. According to the song, they've been together since way back when, and, as they say several times, they're still.....
  A havin' fun
  B gettin' down
  C blowing pot
  D walking the line   {97% correct on the Internet}

14. Another 1976 hit with a TV connection was WELCOME BACK, by John Sebastian. This song hit No.1 and was the theme song for the show "Welcome Back Kotter" (up your nose with a rubber hose!). Complete the line, "we tease him a lot.....
  A and we'll tell him diddly-squat"
  B 'cause we got him on the spot"
  C all his lessons we forgot"
  D this place sure ain't Camelot"   {90% correct on the Internet}

15. In 1977, Linda Ronstadt had what is listed as her only platinum single with a song called BLUE BAYOU. In the beginning of this song, we find out that Linda feels so bad, has a worried mind and feels lonesome all the time, since she.....
  A crossed the Robert E. Lee Natural Bridge
  B left her baby behind on Blue Bayou
  C went down in the boondocks
  D found her baby cheatin'   {87% correct on the Internet}

16. Also in 1977, the Bee Gees hit No. 1 with (excuse us) a very sappy song called HOW DEEP IS YOUR LOVE. But, who are we to say, it was on the charts for six months! Anyway, why do they say they need to know the answer to the title question.....
  A because without love, there is nothing
  B because life's a pain, and then you die
  C because we just couldn't stand a broken heart
  D because they're living in a world of fools   {79% correct on the Internet}

17. On to 1978! A double-dipper for the O'Jays, this time with a song called USE TA BE MY GIRL, a gold record and an R&B No. 1 for five weeks. Yes, if they had the chance, they would take her back! According to this song, the girl's got.....
   A a social disease
   B everything I need
   C nothing to speak of, but, what the heck
   D plenty good lovin'   {30% correct on the Internet}

18. Also in 1978, Queen had a platinum single, with a song called WE ARE THE CHAMPIONS. With "We Will Rock You" on the flip side, this single has become pretty familiar. Anyway, we are the champions, my friends, and what will we do.....?
   A jump, go ahead and jump
   B go to Disneyland
   C keep on fighting to the end
   D rock on, all night long   {98% correct on the Internet}

19. It's 1979, already! That year, Bad Company had a gold record with ROCK 'N' ROLL FANTASY. Try to remember the very beginning of the song to fill in the blank, "here come the _____, one, two, three".....
   A jokecrackers
   B cool dudes
   C jesters
   D brides   {81% correct on the Internet}

20. Last one (don't tell anyone but we made it through the 70s without a disco song!). Peaches & Herb had a platinum single in 1979 with REUNITED. Complete the beginning lines, "I was a fool to ever leave your side, me minus you....."
   A will really crush my pride
   B is really a bummer
   C is such a lonely ride
   D makes a great divide   {89% correct on the Internet}

GAME 5 - 70s SONG THEMES

Here you go with a little bit of these lyrics, and a little bit of those.....remembering the tune will help.

1. WOMEN --- She lives her life inside her room and makes wishes that never come true...
   A Angie Baby by Helen Reddy
   B Delta Dawn by Helen Reddy
   C Jackie Blue by Ozark Mountain Daredevils
   D Dark Lady by Cher   {44% correct on the Internet}

2. AND MORE WOMEN --- The singer tried to make it on Sunday, but got depressed, so he looked ahead to Monday. And a certain woman has been on his mind...
   A Sister Golden Hair by America
   B Sentimental Lady by Bob Welch
   C Sara Smile by Daryl Hall and John Oates
   D My Sharona by Knack   {76% correct on the Internet}

3. COOL DUDES --- You decide who the singer is talking about: There's "talk on the street" about this "Johnny-come-lately"....
   A Hot Stuff by Donna Summer
   B The Rapper by Jaggerz
   C New Kid in Town by the Eagles
   D The Entertainer by Marvin Hamlisch   {49% correct on the Internet}

4. AND MORE COOL DUDES --- Who's the man who is like the dark of night when the moon is shining bright? He's "the man of the hour" with "an air of great power" and he's a "cat of the slum"...
   A Amos Moses by Jerry Reed
   B Magic Man by Heart
   C Superfly by Curtis Mayfield
   D Sir Duke by Stevie Wonder
   E Brother Louie by Stories   {59% correct on the Internet}

5. HOT DUDETTES --- Who's a wild angel, a stranger, dressed in black, running wild, looking pretty?...
   A Devil Woman by Cliff Richard
   B Witchy Woman by the Eagles
   C Evil Woman by the Electric Light Orchestra
   D Hot Child in the City by Nick Gilder
   E Sylvia's Mother by Dr. Hook   {63% correct on the Internet}

6. AND HOTTER(?) DUDETTES --- The singer was working for the FBI downtown on Saturday night when he saw a pair of 45's and experienced a sudden rise in temperature. Who did this to him??
   A Green-Eyed Lady by Sugarloaf
   B Sweet City Woman by the Stampeders
   C Long Cool Woman by the Hollies
   D Cleanup Woman by Betty Wright   {68% correct on the Internet}

7. HAPPINESS! --- Sunday to Saturday, the singer was rockin' all week with you! He says hi to the sunshine and goodbye to the rain, because the girl is wearing his school ring on her chain...
   A I Just Want To Celebrate by Rare Earth
   B Happy Days by Pratt and McClain
   C Some Kind of Wonderful by Grand Funk
   D Feels So Good by Chuck Mangione   {66% correct on the Internet}

8. WHERE ARE WE? --- This is a message to a young man, who is reminded that he needn't feel down, that there's a place he can go and hang out with all the boys...
   A Psychedelic Shack by the Temptations
   B Wild World by Cat Stevens
   C In the Navy by the Village People
   D YMCA by the Village People   {86% correct on the Internet}

9. ROCKIN' ROCK --- Which rocker is looking real hard for a job, and in fact went through Phoenix, Tacoma, Philadelphia, Atlanta, and L.A.?
   A Rock and Roll by Gary Glitter
   B Rock'n Me by Steve Miller
   C Rock Me Gently by Andy Kim

D Rock On by David Essex
   E Rock Your Baby by George McCrae   {82% correct on the Internet}

10. TWOSOMES (or THREESOMES) --- Who are the two that have something going on? They both know that it's wrong, but they meet every day at 6:30 at a cafe anyway...
   A Me and Mrs. Jones by Billy Paul
   B Me and Bobby McGee by Janis Joplin
   C You and Me by Alice Cooper
   D Me and You and a Dog Named Boo by Lobo   {83% correct on the Internet}

11. THE UNWANTED --- Who or what should stay away from the singer, and shouldn't hang around his door? He doesn't even want to see his/her/its/their shadow any more...
   A War by Edwin Starr
   B Backstabbers by the O'Jays
   C Evil Woman by the Electric Light Orchestra
   D American Woman by the Guess Who   {79% correct on the Internet}

12. HOT HOT HOT --- In this informative song, the "heat was hot" and there was a "heart made of ground"....
   A Hot Stuff by Donna Summer
   B Something's Burning by Kenny Rogers and the First Edition
   C A Horse With No Name by America
   D Dust In The Wind by Kansas
   E Wildfire by Michael Murphey   {82% correct on the Internet}

13. SICKNESS --- This singer's really in bad shape: "revved up like a deuce" and in "the dumps with the mumps," he sings about a calliope crashing to the ground! What's the ailment?
   A Blinded by the Light by Manfred Mann
   B Double Vision by Foreigner
   C Rockin' Pneumonia and the Boogie Woogie Flu by Johnny Rivers
   D Bad Case of Loving You by Robert Palmer   {79% correct on the Internet}

14. MORE SICKNESS --- The object of the singer's ill feeling is willing to sacrifice their love and not willing to take advice, but someday will "pay the price." What's wrong with him/her?
   A Hot Blooded by Foreigner
   B Lowdown by Boz Scaggs
   C Cold As Ice by Foreigner
   D Bad Blood by Neil Sedaka   {84% correct on the Internet}

15. SEXIST ATTITUDE --- The singer went through about a million lovers...he/she just loves them and then leaves them alone. What song is it in?
   A Mr. Big Stuff by Jean Knight
   B Oh Girl by the Chi-Lites
   C Fooled Around and Fell In Love by Elvin Bishop
   D You're So Vain by Carly Simon
   E Baby Don't Get Hooked On Me by Mac Davis   {48% correct on the Internet}

16. LET'S CATCH A WAVE --- 73 men set sail from the San Francisco bay, and here's what they had to say:
   A Sail On by the Commodores
   B Come Sail Away by Styx
   C Drift Away by Dobie Gray
   D Float On by the Floaters
   E Ride Captain Ride by Blues Image   {71% correct on the Internet}

17. MOVING FAST NOW --- Tick Tock, Tick Tock. Time keeps "slipping into the future." The singer wants to do this so he/she can save the world:
   A Rise by Herb Alpert
   B Take It To The Limit by the Eagles
   C Fly Like an Eagle by Steve Miller
   D Go Your Own Way by Fleetwood Mac
   E Gonna Fly Now by Bill Conti   {88% correct on the Internet}

18. LOVE SONGS --- The singer asks you to have mercy on her, a poor girl, because she's falling at your feet and tingling from head to toe. When the loving begins the lights will dim...
   A Say You Love Me by Fleetwood Mac
   B I Want Your Love by Chic
   C Love Will Keep Us Together by The Captain and Tennille
   D Love Me by Yvonne Elliman   {75% correct on the Internet}

19. HURTIN' LOVE --- This singer's in trouble because of a "rambler and a gambler and a sweet-talkin' lady's man." And so the singer says this:
   A Love Hurts by Nazareth
   B Help Me by Joni Mitchell
   C Pick Up The Pieces by AWB
   D Don't Leave Me This Way by Thelma Houston   {60% correct on the Internet}

20. AND FINALLY: THE PARTY ANIMALS --- On the road for 40 days, they come into your town and help you party down...
   A Bennie And The Jets by Elton John
   B Sultans of Swing by Dire Straits
   C Band On The Run by Paul McCartney
   D We're An American Band by Grand Funk
   E Boys Are Back In Town by Thin Lizzie   {69% correct on the Internet}

GAME 6 - MORE 70s SONG THEMES

If you love lyrics and want a challenge, here's a game for you.

1. What does the singer NEED in this one? "I rode my bicycle past your window last night.... you got something I need...."
   A Band Of Gold by Freda Payne
   B Brand New Key by Melanie
   C Love Machine by the Miracles
   D Magnet And Steel by Walter Egan
   E My Ding-a-ling by Chuck Berry   {77% correct on the Internet}

2. The singer is making a PLEA here -- what is it? "Heya, heya, what's the matter with your hair...."
   A Come And Get Your Love by Redbone
   B Don't Cry Out Loud by Melissa Manchester
   C Don't Leave Me This Way by Thelma Houston
   D I Want You To Want Me by Cheap Trick   {73% correct on the Internet}

3. What is the REQUEST made by this singer? "Do me wrong, do me right, tell me lies but hold me tight..."
   A Don't Give Up On Us by David Soul
   B Don't Leave Me This Way by Thelma Houston
   C Don't Let Me Be Lonely Tonight by James Taylor
   D Don't Pull Your Love by Hamilton, Joe Frank and Reynolds
   E Don't Stop by Fleetwood Mac   {61% correct on the Internet}

4. What is the DEPRESSING MESSAGE of the song that formulates a new law of the cosmos with the statement "Nothing lasts forever but the earth and sky...."
   A Dust In The Wind by Kansas
   B Isn't It A Pity by George Harrison
   C Lonely Days by the Bee Gees
   D Lonely People by America
   E Rainy Days And Mondays by the Carpenters   {79% correct on the Internet}

5. What RAINY DAY lament is posed by the singer: "...I've seen lonely times when I could not find a friend..."
   A Fire And Rain by James Taylor
   B Have You Ever Seen The Rain by Creedence Clearwater Revival
   C In The Rain by the Dramatics
   D It Never Rains In Southern California by Albert Hammond
   E Laughter In The Rain by Neil Sedaka   {88% correct on the Internet}

6. This singer is FEELIN' BAD. And the song title will sum it up: "Out of work, I'm out of my head...I'm underloved, I'm underfed. I wanna go home."
   A Ain't No Sunshine by Bill Withers
   B Heartache Tonight by the Eagles
   C It Never Rains In Southern California by Albert Hammond
   D It's A Heartache by Bonnie Tyler
   E Raindrops Keep Fallin' On My Head by B. J. Thomas {55% correct on the Internet}

7. HOW should things be, according to this song? "Don't go changing to try and please me....I took the good times, I'll take the bad times...."
   A It Don't Come Easy by Ringo Starr
   B Just The Way You Are by Billy Joel
   C Some Kind Of Wonderful by Grand Funk
   D That's The Way I Like It by KC and the Sunshine Band
   E With A Little Luck by Wings   {92% correct on the Internet}

8. WHEN was this? "Do you remember?".....the singer danced on the night of the 21st; as the stars stole the night away...."
   A December 1963 by the Four Seasons
   B September by Earth, Wind and Fire
   C Summer by War
   D Summer Nights by John Travolta and Olivia Newton-John
   E Sundown by Gordon Lightfoot   {53% correct on the Internet}

9. We're really ROCKIN' now, but on what rock? "...see her shake on the movie screen, Jimmy Dean!"
   A Rock Me Gently by Andy Kim
   B Rock On by David Essex

C Rock The Boat by Hues Corporation
   D Rock Your Baby by George McCrae
   E Rockin' Me by Steve Miller   {81% correct on the Internet}

10. Some sentimental nostalgia in this song. WHAT could be the object of its words? "We walked to the sea, just my father and me, and the dogs played around on the sand..."
   A Drift Away by Dobie Gray
   B Escape by Rupert Holmes
   C Reminiscing by the Little River Band
   D Ships by Barry Manilow
   E Still Water by the Four Tops   {40% correct on the Internet}

11. WHERE did this one come from? "...my poor mother worked the mines. I was raised on the good book, Jesus..."
   A Back Home Again by John Denver
   B Right Back Where We Started From by Maxine Nightingale
   C Still Water by the Four Tops
   D Stoney End by Barbra Streisand
   E Sweet Home Alabama by Lynyrd Skynyrd   {35% correct on the Internet}

12. A GREETING of sorts in this song: "Hello, how are you? Have you been alright through all those lonely, lonely, lonely, lonely, lonely nights?..."
   A Goodbye To Love by the Carpenters
   B Hello It's Me by Todd Rundgren
   C Never Can Say Goodbye by the Jackson 5
   D Telephone Line by the Electric Light Orchestra
   E When Will I See You Again by Three Degrees   {64% correct on the Internet}

13. Just WHEN does the singer do what these words say? "...miles and miles of empty space in between us....it's cold out, but hold out, and do like I do...."
   A Before The Next Teardrop Falls by Freddy Fender
   B Day After Day by Badfinger
   C Right Time Of The Night by Jennifer Warnes

   D Sometimes When We Touch by Dan Hill
   E When I Need You by Leo Sayer   {77% correct on the Internet}

14. WHO is being referred to in this song? "...Live a little, be a gypsy, get around. Get your feet up off the ground...."
   A Gypsy Man by War
   B Gypsy Woman by Brian Hyland
   C Magic Man by Heart
   D Sultans Of Swing by Dire Straits
   E Uncle Albert / Admiral Halsey by Paul and Linda McCartney
                                              {59% correct on the Internet}

15. Someone needs HELP in this song: "When you're weary, feeling small, when tears are in your eyes I will dry them all..."
   A Bridge Over Troubled Water by Simon and Garfunkel
   B He Ain't Heavy, He's My Brother by the Hollies
   C I Can Help by Billy Swan
   D Love Will Keep Us Together by the Captain and Tennille
   E You've Got A Friend by James Taylor   {78% correct on the Internet}

16. What WEATHER CONDITION is suggested by this song? "If I could make a wish I think I'd pass....so sleep, silent angel, go to sleep....sometimes all I need is...."
   A Air That I Breathe by the Hollies
   B Smoke On The Water by Deep Purple
   C Summer Breeze by Seals and Crofts
   D Sunshine by Jonathan Edwards
   E Sunshine On My Shoulders by John Denver   {80% correct on the Internet}

17. Sort of an ODD name for sort of an odd song: "When I think back on all the crap I learned in high school, it's a wonder I can think at all..."
   A Bang A Gong by T Rex
   B Chick-A-Boom by Daddy Dewdrop
   C Kodachrome by Paul Simon
   D My Ding-A-Ling by Chuck Berry
   E Yoyo by the Osmonds   {81% correct on the Internet}

18. A SAD story here: "They got a name for the winners of the world. They call Alabama the Crimson Tide." But what about me?
　A Bluer Than Blue by Michael Johnson
　B Deacon Blues by Steely Dan
　C I Go Crazy by Paul Davis
　D Lowdown by Boz Scaggs
　E Sad Eyes by Robert John　　　　{61% correct on the Internet}

19. How HIGH are they goin': "...Teachers, keep on teachin'. Preachers, keep on preachin'. World, keep on turnin'...."
　A Higher And Higher by Rita Coolidge
　B Higher Ground by Stevie Wonder
　C Outa-Space by Billy Preston
　D Sky High by Jigsaw
　E Top Of The World by the Carpenters　　{62% correct on the Internet}

20. This singer is really trying to get something. WHAT is it? "I've been to Hollywood, I've been to Redwood, I crossed the ocean" for this....
　A An Everlasting Love by Carl Carlton
　B Band Of Gold by Freda Payne
　C Fame by David Bowie
　D Heart Of Gold by Neil Young
　E Natural High by Bloodstone　　{83% correct on the Internet}

GAME 7 - SUBTITLES FROM THE 70s

Each of these songs had an "official" subtitle. All you have to do is pick out what it was.

1. In 1970, the song INSTANT KARMA achieved gold record status. The artist is listed as John Ono Lennon. George Harrison played guitar. The subtitle is.....
   A ('S Gonna Get You)
   B (Give Peace A Chance)
   C (We All Shine On)
   D (Ohmmmmmm)   {65% correct on the Internet}

2. The highest rated 70s song with a subtitle is DECEMBER, 1963 by The Four Seasons. Recorded by a group of singers much different from the 1960s, it became their best-selling single. The subtitle is.....
   A (Oh, What A Night)
   B (A Winter Wonderland)
   C (There She Was)
   D (Time Of The Seasons)   {91% correct on the Internet}

3. Gilbert O'Sullivan had several hits in the 70s, but his first was ALONE AGAIN, a song that would have to make the top ten of the most depressing songs ever. The subtitle is.....
   A (Without You)
   B (Naturally)
   C (Don't You See)
   D (Frequently)   {80% correct on the Internet}

4. A group of thirty-four studio musicians recorded TSOP in 1973, and it was first used as the theme song for Soul Train. The artist was listed as MFSB, or "Mother Father Sister Brother". The subtitle for TSOP is.....
   A (The Singers On Parade)
   B (The Sound Of Philadelphia)
   C (That Sweet Old Place)
   D (The Soul Of the People)   {60% correct on the Internet}

5. In 1971, The Raiders had a gold record called INDIAN RESERVATION. Almost released as a solo by Mark Lindsey, it was the Raiders' (as in Paul Revere and) biggest hit. The subtitle is.....
   A (The Trail Of Tears)
   B (Indian Territory, My Foot!)
   C (The Lament Of The Cherokee Reservation Indian)
   D (The Ghost Dance Song)   {74% correct on the Internet}

6. In 1972, The Hollies had their highest-charting song, with LONG COOL WOMAN. Yes, you probably already know the answer, but the subtitle is.....
   A (How I Dig You)
   B (In An Itsy-Bitsy Teenie-Weenie Yellow Polka-Dot Bikini)
   C (In A Black Dress)
   D (Do You Love Me)   {91% correct on the Internet}

7. How about "one-hit wonder" Edison Lighthouse, who scored big in 1970 with LOVE GROWS. This was a British studio group and the song made it to No. 5. The subtitle is.....
   A (I Would Like To Disclose)
   B (Where My Rosemary Goes)
   C (Where The Long River Flows)
   D (When She Plays The Banjo)   {84% correct on the Internet}

8. In 1977, Bill Conti had a No. 1 hit and a gold record, but you might need to know your movies to get this one. The song is GONNA FLY NOW and the subtitle is.....
   A (Theme From "Karate Kid")
   B (Theme From "A Summer Place")
   C (Theme From "Shaft")
   D (Theme From "Rocky")   {87% correct on the Internet}

9. A group called Looking Glass had a big hit in 1972 called Brandy. It was based on a real person, but a mostly fictional situation (you know.....the sailors and all). Anyway, the subtitle is.....
   A (Lay That Whiskey Down)
   B (Gee, You're Swell)
   C (You're A Fine Girl)
   D (Loves The Sea, Not Me)   {89% correct on the Internet}

10. In 1977, Barbra Streisand had one of the top five songs of the year with LOVE THEME FROM "A STAR IS BORN". She wrote the song with composer Paul Williams. You may know the song by it's subtitle, which is.....
 A (Forever)
 B (Disco Nights)
 C (Evermore)
 D (Evergreen)   {81% correct on the Internet}

11. In 1976, Rod Stewart had Billboard's No. 1 song for the year with TONIGHT'S THE NIGHT. It was a controversial song because of its sexual connotations and it was banned in some places. It's subtitle is.....
 A (Gonna Be Alright)
 B (Things Look So Bright)
 C (Don't Be Uptight)
 D (Yes, You're A Neophyte)   {95% correct on the Internet}

12. Rupert Holmes had a No. 1 song in 1979 called ESCAPE. It kind of foreshadowed the personal ad craze.....the woman he met turned out to be his girlfriend.....remember? The subtitle for this one is.....
 A (Oh, What A Surprise!)
 B (I Never Knew)
 C (Pina Colada Song)
 D (Making Love At Midnight)   {79% correct on the Internet}

13. Another "one-hit wonder," Alicia Bridges, scored big in 1978 with the disco tune I LOVE THE NIGHTLIFE (be careful on this one). The subtitle is.....
 A (I Got To Boogie)
 B (Is That Bar Open?)
 C (We'll Get It On, Now)
 D (Disco 'Round)   {23% correct on the Internet}

14. Marilyn McCoo and Billy Davis, Jr., who were married and members of the 5th Dimension, had a gold record in 1977 with YOU DON'T HAVE TO BE A STAR. The subtitle is.....
 A (And I'll Never Go Far)

B (To Me You Just Glow)
   C (I Want You To Know)
   D (To Be In My Show) {90% correct on the Internet}

15. In 1970, The Temptations had started to go relevant and they had a big hit with BALL OF CONFUSION. The song made it to No. 3 and had a subtitle that might be tough to remember. It is.....
   A (That's What The World Is Today)
   B (Makes Me Wanna Holler)
   C (Can't We All Just Get Along?)
   D (And The Band Played On) {58% correct on the Internet}

16. In 1976, Diana Ross had a No. 1 song called THEME FROM MAHOGANY. It was, of course, from the movie Mahogany, which had Ross in a starring role. The rather long subtitle is.....
   A (What's It All About, My Love)
   B (Tell Me, What Am I Living For)
   C (Does Anyone Really Know What Time It Is)
   D (Do You Know Where You're Going To) {83% correct on the Internet}

17. The first big hit for Melanie was called LAY DOWN, which hit No. 6 in 1970. It was a powerful song, helped by vocals from The Edwin Hawkins Singers. The rather unique subtitle is.....
   A (Brand New Key)
   B (Bright Purple Flowers)
   C (Candles In The Rain)
   D (But Not In The Middle Of The Street) {56% correct on the Internet}

18. Another song with a rather unique subtitle was the 1973 gold record LEAVE ME ALONE, by Helen Reddy, who had a number of big hits in the early 70s. The subtitle is.....
   A (Babe In The Wood)
   B (Ruby Red Dress)
   C (Tie The Lover's Knot)
   D (Pip, Squeak And Wilfred) {70% correct on the Internet}

19. The only performers to make this quiz twice are The Temptations. In 1971, they got away from the relevant "musical messages" and hit No. 1 with JUST MY IMAGINATION. The subtitle is.....
  A (Things We Said Today)
  B (Or Was It A Dream?)
  C (Or Wasn't It Smokey Robinson & The Miracles?)
  D (Running Away With Me)   {87% correct on the Internet}

20. The last question is kind of a stumper, since it's about a song from 1975 that wasn't a real big hit, but it had a strange subtitle. Mac Davis made it to No. 15 with a song called ROCK N' ROLL. Kudos if you know the subtitle.....
  A (Does Your Chewing Gum Lose It's Flavor On The Bedpost Overnight?)
  B (It's The One Thing That Has Kept Me Together)
  C (I Gave You The Best Years Of My Life)
  D (Let's Play It All.....All Night Long)   {48% correct on the Internet}

GAME 8 - WHAT 70s SONG WAS THAT?

I hope you're not expecting a bunch of disco songs here.....if so, sorry to disappoint you. What was that line again.....Disco _ _ _ _ _ ?

1. The singer is looking forward to catching up on his reading, running through the house screaming, and having a lot more room in his closet. But what's the real scenario here?
   A Lonely Days by the Bee Gees
   B Lonely People by America
   C You're Only Lonely by J. D. Souther
   D Sad Eyes by Robert John
   E Bluer Than Blue by Michael Johnson   {41% correct on the Internet}

2. This former member of the Kingston Trio sang "when the lights go down in the California town"....he jumps into his car, bringing his guitar. And then, he/she mentions the subject of this song:
   A Gold by John Stewart
   B Band Of Gold by Freda Payne
   C Dancing In The Moonlight by King Harvest
   D Swaying To The Music by Johnny Rivers   {47% correct on the Internet}

3. Never a #1 song but 40 weeks on the charts! The singer laments that it's been a long time getting over the lost love....they could be friends, but..."my heart just can't hide that ol' feeling inside..."
   A It's A Heartache by Bonnie Tyler
   B Heartache Tonight by the Eagles
   C I Go Crazy by Paul Davis
   D Bad Case of Loving You by Robert Palmer   {68% correct on the Internet}

4. This one has eye problems. He's feeling mean. He says, "It's time I had a good time, ain't got time to wait". Eventually, he won't be able to see straight.
   A Doctor My Eyes by Jackson Browne
   B I Can See Clearly Now by Johnny Nash

  C Blinded By The Light by Manfred Mann's Earth Band
  D Double Vision by Foreigner   {68% correct on the Internet}

5. And this one's a real sicko. The singer says: "I got a fever of a hundred and three..", and wants to meet after the show...looking for a secret rendezvous...
  A Hot Blooded by Foreigner
  B Night Fever by the Bee Gees
  C Jungle Fever by Chakachas
  D Love Hangover by Diana Ross
  E Rockin' Pneumonia And The Boogie Woogie Flu by Johnny Rivers   {87% correct on the Internet}

6. This song talks about a Bogart movie...about a lady "with a silk dress running, like a water color in the rain"...and, the drum is beating. Exactly when does this all happen?
  A Hollywood Nights by Bob Seger
  B Golden Years by David Bowie
  C Year Of The Cat by Al Stewart
  D Summer Nights by John Travolta and Olivia Newton-John
     {57% correct on the Internet}

7. This song would first come-a come-a come-along in 1960 when Jimmy Jones did it. Not the kind to use the pencil or rule, the singer just knew how to fix broken hearts (24 hours a day, if necessary):
  A Handy Man by James Taylor
  B I Can Help by Billy Swan
  C I'll Be There by the Jackson 5
  D Hello It's Me by Todd Rundgren   {81% correct on the Internet}

8. The singer would be leaving at dawn...for the green on the other side of the hill...he was "born a wrangler and a rambler..." Careful here.....think about it!
  A Ramblin Man by the Allman Brothers Band
  B Ramblin' Gamblin' Man by the Bob Seger System
  C Natural High by Bloodstone
  D Heard It In A Love Song by the Marshall Tucker Band
     {44% correct on the Internet}

9. Sort of a mellow one here. The singer believes that "you can get me through the night".....he wants to be flown through the skies...to the bright side of the moon...
   A Don't Fear The Reaper by Blue Oyster Cult
   B Dream Weaver by Gary Wright
   C Spirit In The Sky by Norman Greenbaum
   D Undercover Angel by Alan O'Day
   E Angel In Your Arms by Hot   {85% correct on the Internet}

10. Don't get hooked by this one. She's Jamaican, works on Lexington, she's a tall girl, standing over 6 feet..."turning tricks for the dudes..."
   A The Bitch Is Back by Elton John
   B Island Girl by Elton John
   C Lady Marmalade by LaBelle
   D Lady Blue by Leon Russell
   E Rich Girl by Hall & Oates   {57% correct on the Internet}

11. Allegedly about drugs, this song has the words "All around in my home town, they're trying to track me down." But the singer professes innocence!
   A Renegade by Styx
   B I Shot The Sheriff by Eric Clapton
   C Indiana Wants Me by R. Dean Taylor
   D Lonesome Loser by the Little River Band   {89% correct on the Internet}

12. In this song, the singer spun fortune wheels, left home at 13, and said "you can have your funky world."
   A Ramblin' Gamblin' Man by the Bob Seger System
   B Ramblin Man by the Allman Brothers Band
   C Gypsy Man by War
   D The Gambler by Kenny Rogers
   E Half-Breed by Cher   {71% correct on the Internet}

13. It seems that this train will definitely be stopping in England....."tell all the folks in Russia and China, too."
   A Love Train by the O'Jays
   B Peace Train by Cat Stevens

   C Long Train Runnin' by the Doobie Brothers
   D Midnight Train To Georgia by Gladys Knight and the Pips
                                  {52% correct on the Internet}

14. When he was a little boy and when he was a man, the devil called his name. What's more, if he were President, this would happen, once Congress called his name....
   A LetYour Love Flow by the Bellamy Brothers
   B Kiss And Say Goodbye by the Manhattans
   C Loves Me Like A Rock by Paul Simon
   D Kiss You All Over by Exile
   E Ring My Bell by Anita Ward   {72% correct on the Internet}

15. What kind of job is this? All that science, cold as hell, not the place to raise your kids, high as a kite by 9 AM!
   A Candy Man by Sammy Davis Jr.
   B Handy Man by James Taylor
   C Poetry Man by Phoebe Snow
   D Rocket Man by Elton John
   E Tin Man by America   {87% correct on the Internet}

16. This son of a minister sang about lines on his face and hands from all his troubles. He
was in the middle without any plans, both a boy and a man...
   A Golden Years by David Bowie
   B Time In A Bottle by Jim Croce
   C Walk On The Wild Side by Lou Reed
   D Eighteen by Alice Cooper   {65% correct on the Internet}

17. Who was the "..ocean lady....passion's lady...."? Apparently, she was also windswept....how may of you like your significant other to be "windswept"?
   A Island Girl by Elton John
   B Green-Eyed Lady by Sugarloaf
   C Long Cool Woman by the Hollies
   D Dark Lady by Cher
   E Cleanup Woman by Betty Wright   {71% correct on the Internet}

18. Referring to his previous failures, the singer said "sweet dreams and flying machines in
pieces on the ground." And poor "Suzanne"!
   A In The Rain by the Dramatics
   B Ain't No Sunshine by Bill Withers
   C Fire And Rain by James Taylor
   D Lowdown by Boz Scaggs
   E I Go Crazy by Paul Davis   {68% correct on the Internet}

19. This song was by a hippie chicken farmer near San Francisco. He sang of dying, being able to rest, going to the place that's the best. "Never been a sinner -- never sinned -- I got a friend in Jesus."
   A Spirit In The Sky by Norman Greenbaum
   B Angel In Your Arms by Hot
   C Don't Fear The Reaper by Blue Oyster Cult
   D Gonna Fly Now by Bill Conti
   E Amos Moses by Jerry Reed   {88% correct on the Internet}

20. Randy Newman wrote this about an extra crazy party. Don't turn on the lights, because the singer doesn't want to see what's there! "That ain't the way to have fun, son."
   A Lowdown by Boz Scaggs
   B I Just Wanna Stop by Gino Vannelli
   C Help Me by Joni Mitchell
   D Spill The Wine by Eric Burdon and War
   E Mama Told Me Not To Come by Three Dog Night   {80% correct on the Internet}

GAME 9 - 70s VARIETY

Quick questions about some of the more popular songs of the 70s.

1. Which was not one of Paul Simon's "fifty ways to leave your lover"?
    A Drop off the key, Lee
    B Make a new plan, Stan
    C Get out of bed, Fred
    D Slip out the back, Jack   {81% correct on the Internet}

2. Someone's in trouble with the authorities here. The song in question has a catchy part at the end with a "beep beep" and a series of police whistles:
    A Undercover Angel
    B I Shot the Sheriff
    C Bad Girls
    D Indiana Wants Me   {48% correct on the Internet}

3. Saturday's a happy day, right? Not if you ain't got nobody to talk to, even with your paycheck in your pocket:
    A Saturday Night
    B Saturday Night's Alright for Fighting
    C Saturday in the Park
    D Another Saturday Night
    E Come Saturday Morning   {77% correct on the Internet}

4. And rainy days can really get you down. In which of these does the singer lament that "it's raining all over the world"?
    A Rainy Night in Georgia
    B Rainy Days and Mondays
    C Rainy Day People
    D Raindrops Keep Fallin' on My Head
    E It Never Rains in Southern California   {48% correct on the Internet}

5. Neil Young's Sugar Mountain had this:
    A Candy treats for everyone
    B Trees alive a thousand years

   C Barkers and colored balloons
   D A heart of gold   {44% correct on the Internet}

6. Fat chance that any of these song titles will come true. But which one was in a Coke commercial?
   A People Got To Be Free
   B I'll Never Fall in Love Again
   C Baby, Don't Get Hooked on Me
   D I Write the Songs (That Make the Whole World Sing)
   E I'd Like To Teach the World To Sing   {93% correct on the Internet}

7. In "Joy to the World," Three Dog Night offers up joy not only to the whole world, but also to the:
   A only one who sets me free
   B angels singing harmony
   C birdies and the mama bee
   D fishes in the deep blue sea   {92% correct on the Internet}

8. WHERE am I when I "give up the booze and the one-night stands," and plan to live in a nice, quiet little town?
   A Copacabana
   B YMCA
   C Hotel California
   D Baker Street
   E Mainstreet   {66% correct on the Internet}

9. Who or what was ultimately to blame for the singer's condition in Jimmy Buffett's "Margaritaville"?
   A A bartender
   B A woman
   C Society
   D The singer himself
   E Low scores on the trivia quiz   {63% correct on the Internet}

10. "A hustle here, and a hustle there, New York City is the place" where you:
   A Escape
   B Shake Your Booty

C Take a Walk on the Wild Side
D Do the Hustle
E Ring My Bell   {66% correct on the Internet}

11. In Harry Chapin's ballad "Taxi," 2 ex-lovers are reunited, after many years, in the singer's taxi. As the story unfolds, we learn that she and he had failed in their dreams to become:
A an actress and a pilot
B a singer and a doctor
C a dancer and a ballplayer
D convenience store clerks   {57% correct on the Internet}

12. In this place the rose only comes up "when the moon is on the run and all the stars are gleaming."
A Arizona
B Indian Reservation
C Sweet Home Alabama
D Spanish Harlem
E YMCA   {58% correct on the Internet}

13. The singer refers to a girl who makes his dreams come true. "Out of all the fellas in the world, she belongs to you." This is all about:
A Emotion
B Reminiscing
C Just My Imagination
D A Peaceful Easy Feeling
E Love's Theme   {56% correct on the Internet}

14. When the singer of this song is feeling lonely and beat, he drifts back in time and finds his feet...where the pool halls, hustlers, and losers are:
A Mainstreet
B Baker Street
C On Broadway
D Thunder Island
E YMCA   {64% correct on the Internet}

15. In "The Joker," the Steve Miller Band had a rather unusual way of expressing their affection. The singer...
   A Likes a kitty, so will pull your tail
   B Likes his tea with sugar, so will drink you up
   C Likes your peaches, so will shake your tree
   D Likes his candy kisses, so will nibble on you   {91% correct on the Internet}

16. "It was against the law, what the mama saw." But the "radical priest" will help, and they'll end up on the cover of Newsweek.
   A Me and Mrs. Jones
   B Me and You and a Dog Named Boo
   C Me and Bobby McGee
   D Me and Julio Down By the Schoolyard   {66% correct on the Internet}

17. In this song "paradise" is paved over with a parking lot:
   A Reminiscing
   B Big Yellow Taxi
   C Ventura Highway
   D Top of the World
   E Car Wash   {63% correct on the Internet}

18. Which is NOT one of the catchy tunes of KC and the Sunshine Band?
   A Get Down Tonight
   B That's the Way I Like It
   C Shake Your Booty
   D Jive Talkin'
   E I'm Your Boogie Man   {82% correct on the Internet}

19. According to King Harvest, "Dancing in the Moonlight" is a:
   A Rhythmic flow of light
   B Psychedelic sight
   C Supernatural delight
   D High-producing rite
   E Lunar body night   {68% correct on the Internet}

20. Papa may have been a rolling stone, but he was a bad dude, too. Which of these is NOT said of old pops in the Temptations song?
   A He had 3 outside children and another wife
   B He did some time working for the man on the chain gang
   C He was a storefront preacher, stealing in the name of the Lord
   D He spent most of his time chasing women and drinking
   E He called himself a jack of all trades   {35% correct on the Internet}

GAME 10 - THE SNEAKY 70s

If you like challenges, this game is for you....it's one of the tougher ones, even though there are only three possible answers for each question!

1. The first question for this game is the 1971 song RINGS from the one-hit wonder Cymarron. The song is all about doorbells, telephones and wedding bells. When his girlfriend comes in the house, which artist is playing on the stereo?
   A Jim Morrison
   B Smokey Robinson
   C James Taylor   {34% correct on the Internet}

2. Next one is from another one-hit wonder, Sammy Johns, who scored with CHEVY VAN in 1975. You know the story of the hitchhiker that he picks up, and he drops her off in her town which was so small.....
   A "I was through it in a wink of an eye"
   B "everyone saw her come home"
   C "you could throw a rock from end to end"   {45% correct on the Internet}

3. Don McLean's VINCENT was written about
   A his brother Vincent
   B Vincent Van Gogh
   C Leonardo da Vinci   {47% correct on the Internet}

4. Arlo Guthrie had a hit in 1972 with a tribute to the railroad called THE CITY OF NEW ORLEANS. The song tells a very nice story with lots of details, but the question is how far the train has gone "when the day is done".....
   A 500 miles
   B 300 miles
   C 700 miles   {84% correct on the Internet}

5. In 1974, Lynyrd Skynyrd had their biggest hit with SWEET HOME ALABAMA. In the song, they mention a major event, and whether or not it might give one a "guilty conscience". It was.....
   A Watergate
   B integration
   C Vietnam War   {59% correct on the Internet}

6. LaBelle sang about Lady Marmalade in 1975. In what city did Llady M say, "Hey Joe, you wanna give it a go?"
   A Fairbanks
   B New York
   C New Orleans   {71% correct on the Internet}

7. Al Stewart, though not nearly as prolific as Rod, had a couple of big hits in the late 70s. His first, YEAR OF THE CAT, is about a mysterious woman who says she came from that year. In the beginning of the song, he mentions a famous actor. Who?
   A Humphrey Bogart
   B Peter Lorre
   C John Wayne   {37% correct on the Internet}

8. In 1977, Paul Simon had a big hit with SLIP SLIDIN' AWAY. He mentions only one name in the song, a woman who was loved powerfully by a man he knew. Her name? (hint: there is a connection to a Seinfeld episode).....
   A Nancy
   B Delores
   C Jenny   {82% correct on the Internet}

9. In Gordon Lightfoot's IF YOU COULD READ MY MIND, which of these does the singer NOT compare his mind to?
   A a paperback novel
   B an old-time movie
   C a faded love letter   {67% correct on the Internet}

10. Also from 1970, the Moments made it all the way to No. 3 with LOVE ON A TWO-WAY STREET. If you remember, that's where they found love, but where did they lose it?
   A on a lonely highway
   B on a one-way street
   C on the road to nowhere   {69% correct on the Internet}

11. If you've been to a wedding lately, you may well have danced to Y.M.C.A. by The Village People. They talk about what a great place the Y is for a young man who is new in town. For most of the song, what is the line right before the refrain Y.M.C.A.?
   A it's fun to stay at the.....
   B all you come to the.....
   C see you all at the.....   {94% correct on the Internet}

12. Still another Stewart to ask about, this time John, who had his song GOLD make it to No. 5 in 1979. It's all about the people out there (I guess John is one of them) and what they are turning into gold. What is it?
   A love
   B anything
   C music   {71% correct on the Internet}

13. In 1973, Grand Funk Railroad had the first of their two No. 1 hits with WE'RE AN AMERICAN BAND. The song mentions two cities where the band had a great time while stopped on their 40 day tour. Which one is NOT mentioned?
   A Omaha
   B Kansas City
   C Little Rock   {50% correct on the Internet}

14. It's time for another one-hit wonder, this time a group called Stories. Their song, BROTHER LOUIE, made it to No. 1 in 1973. In it, Louie had a problem because of his girlfriend. His family wouldn't accept her because she was.....
   A much older
   B black
   C white   {57% correct on the Internet}

15. Also in 1973, Gladys Knight & The Pips hit No. 1 with MIDNIGHT TRAIN TO GEORGIA. Her man's dreams didn't come true and she is returning to Georgia with him. Where are they leaving from?
   A San Francisco
   B Los Angeles
   C New York   {45% correct on the Internet}

16. By far the biggest hit for The Allman Brothers Band was RAMBLIN MAN, again from 1973. The singer had a life of wandering, his father was a gambler, etc., etc. The song does tell us where he was born, which was.....
   A out in a cottonfield
   B in the backroom of a diner
   C on the back seat of a Greyhound bus   {90% correct on the Internet}

17. Roger Whittaker's LAST FAREWELL recalled the beauty of his homeland. What was it?
   A England
   B Australia
   C Austria   {68% correct on the Internet}

18. Here's one from Elton John.....in 1975, he had a platinum single with ISLAND GIRL. It was the story of a "black as coal" prostitute, and she was a big girl, Elton tells us how tall she was. The answer.....
   A 6'0"
   B 6"5"
   C 6'3"   {79% correct on the Internet}

19. In 1976, a group called Starbuck had a nice-sounding hit called MOONLIGHT FEELS RIGHT. It was all about the singer's encounter at the ocean with an attractive young woman, under the moonlight. Based on where she was from, she was a.....
   A northern girl
   B southern belle
   C California beach baby   {45% correct on the Internet}

20. The final selection for the game is about the 1974 No. 1 song, by Bo Donaldson & The Heywoods, called BILLY, DON'T BE A HERO. Billy, of course, tries to be a hero and ends up being killed. The song implies which war the song was written about.....
  A World War I
  B Vietnam War
  C Civil War   {25% correct on the Internet}

Chapter 4 - The 80s and the 90s

GAME 1 - 80s SONG THEMES

Lyrics can be great, can't they? Well, if you think you know your lyrics, get busy with these......

1. This song has an ATTITUDE: "The landlord say your rent is late, he may have to litigate...."
   A Alive And Kicking by Simple Minds
   B Back To Life by Soul II Soul
   C Don't Worry, Be Happy by Bobby McFerrin
   D Sad Songs by Elton John
   E Trouble by Lindsey Buckingham   {90% correct on the Internet}

2. WHO or WHAT are we talking about? A man walking down the street says "why am I soft in the middle now...who'll be my role-model?"
   A Against All Odds by Phil Collins
   B Family Man by Hall and Oates
   C Man In The Mirror by Michael Jackson
   D Second Chance by Thirty Eight Special
   E You Can Call Me Al by Paul Simon {87% correct on the Internet}

3. The answer's just IMPOSSIBLE! "Strangled by the wishes of pater...I'll keep holding on..."
   A Hold On To The Nights by Richard Marx
   B Holding Back The Years by Simply Red
   C If I Could Turn Back Time by Cher
   D Living Inside Myself by Gino Vannelli
   E Perfect World by Huey Lewis and the News   {64% correct on the Internet}

4. WHERE the heck are we? "A million lights are dancing...a shooting star... neon lights...the dream that came through a million years...."
   A Africa by Toto
   B Desert Moon by Dennis DeYoung
   C Electric Avenue by Eddy Grant
   D Twilight Zone by Golden Earring
   E Xanadu by Olivia Newton-John   {56% correct on the Internet}

5. What's this person's PROBLEM? He/she wakes up with "the sheets soaking wet, and a freight train running thru the middle of my head..."
  A Burning Heart by Survivor
  B Delirious by Prince
  C Heart Attack by Olivia Newton-John
  D Heat Of The Night by Bryan Adams
  E I'm On Fire by Bruce Springsteen   {82% correct on the Internet}

6. Ah, MEMORIES: was it really like this? "Way back when in '67, I was the dandy of Gamma Chi...."
  A Casanova by Levert
  B Could've Been by Tiffany
  C Hey 19 by Steely Dan
  D '65 Love Affair by Paul Davis
  E Summer of '69 by Bryan Adams   {77% correct on the Internet}

7. Ah, MEMORIES II: "teach me how to be sensible, logical, responsible, practical...."
  A Hey 19 by Steely Dan
  B Invincible by Pat Benatar
  C Karma Chameleon by Culture Club
  D Logical Song by Supertramp
  E Through The Years by Kenny Rogers   {87% correct on the Internet}

8. Just PINING AWAY: "I have a picture pinned to my wall....Look at our life now, tattered and torn...."
  A Could've Been by Tiffany
  B Don't Dream It's Over by Crowded House
  C Hold Me Now by the Thompson Twins
  D Lost In Emotion by Lisa Lisa and Cult Jam
  E Miss You Much by Janet Jackson   {53% correct on the Internet}

9. EXOTICA: "...As sure as Kilimanjaro rises like Olympus above the Serangeti..."
  A Africa by Toto
  B Bang A Gong by Power Station
  C Conga by Miami Sound Machine

D Rhythm Of The Night by DeBarge
   E Xanadu by Olivia Newton-John   {90% correct on the Internet}

10. SHE's really got a hold on me: "...Not quite a year since she went away...meet you all the way...meet you all the way..."
   A Amanda by Boston
   B Angelia by Richard Marx
   C Joanna by Kool and the Gang
   D Nikita by Elton John
   E Rosanna by Toto   {77% correct on the Internet}

11. Getting a little SORDID here: "...keep your mind on the money...Deutschmarks or dollars, American Express will do nicely - thank you."
   A Bad Girls by Donna Summer
   B Material Girl by Madonna
   C Naughty Girls by Samantha Fox
   D Point Of No Return by Expose
   E Private Dancer by Tina Turner   {60% correct on the Internet}

12. LOVE this one: "...bring your jukebox money"
   A Love Zone by Billy Ocean
   B Can't Buy Me Love by the Beatles
   C Love Is A Battlefield by Pat Benatar
   D Love Shack by the B-52's
   E You Give Love A Bad Name by Bon Jovi   {91% correct on the Internet}

13. Good EFFORT here: "I have climbed the highest mountains...scaled these city walls...held the hand of a devil..."
   A Against All Odds by Phil Collins
   B Every Little Step by Bobby Brown
   C I Still Haven't Found What I'm Looking For by U2
   D I Want To Know What Love Is by Foreigner
   E Walk On Water by Eddie Money   {87% correct on the Internet}

14. Which one of these individuals or groups had a popular 1986 song with part of his/her/their NAME AS ITS TITLE?
   A Houston by Whitney Houston
   B The Genesis by Genesis
   C Wham! by Wham! featuring George Michael
   D Revolution by Prince & the Revolution
   E Human by the Human League   {77% correct on the Internet}

15. DEPRESSING, but ungrammatical? "....they passed a law in '64 to give those who ain't got a little more..."
   A Against All Odds by Phil Collins
   B All Over The World by Electric Light Orchestra
   C Starting Over by John Lennon
   D The Way It Is by Bruce Hornsby and the Range
   E When The Children Cry by White Lion   {85% correct on the Internet}

16. What's the OCCASION, then? "No New Year's Day....no chocolate covered candy hearts....no April rain..."
   A Always On My Mind by Willie Nelson
   B The Best Of Times by Styx
   C Celebration by Kool and the Gang
   D I Just Called To Say I Love You by Stevie Wonder
   E Nothin' But A Good Time by Poison   {92% correct on the Internet}

17. Gettin' HIGH on this one: "Who knows what tomorrow brings?....the eagles cry on a mountain high..."
   A Eye In The Sky by the Alan Parsons Project
   B Point Of No Return by Expose
   C Somewhere Out There by Linda Ronstadt and James Ingram
   D Straight Up by Paula Abdul
   E Up Where We Belong by Joe Cocker and Jennifer Warnes
                    {90% correct on the Internet}

18. The singer's PLEADING with you: "...you're the only one who really knew me at all...."
   A Against All Odds by Phil Collins
   B Don't Dream It's Over by Crowded House
   C Don't Forget Me by Glass Tiger
   D Don't Let Go by Isaac Hayes
   E Don't Stop Believin' by Journey   {90% correct on the Internet}

19. Whatever the singer's DOING here, we should all do it: "...paradise...tranquility...never-never land...reverie...symphony..."
   A Cruisin' by Smokey Robinson
   B Running With The Night by Lionel Richie
   C Sailing by Christopher Cross
   D Steppin' Out by Joe Jackson
   E Walking On Sunshine by Katrina and the Waves   {68% correct on the Internet}

20. RELIVING THE PAST: "I am older now, I have more than what I wanted..." Do you question all the answers in this one?
   A Could've Been by Tiffany
   B I Still Haven't Found What I'm Looking For by U2
   C I Want To Know What Love Is by Foreigner
   D Things Can Only Get Better by Howard Jones
   E Wasted On The Way by Crosby, Stills, and Nash   {56% correct on the Internet}

GAME 2 - EASY 80s

Not to put pressure on you or anything, but, this game may prove that you know your 80s music.

1. Let's start with the No. 2 song from 1980. It's from the soundtrack of the movie American Gigolo, and Debbie Harry and Blondie give out an assignment. She sings, "when you're ready, we can share the wine", so.....
   A Give Me The Night
   B Take Your Time (Do It Right)
   C Call Me
   D Ring My Bell   {82% correct on the Internet}

2. Another hit from 1980. In this one, Irene Cara wants something real bad. In fact, she's going to learn how to fly, live forever, and make it to heaven, among other things. You just better remember her name, because she wants.....
   A Somebody's Baby
   B Fame
   C Real Love
   D Endless Love   {98% correct on the Internet}

3. Again, 1980. This disco/R&B hit ranked as high as No. 6 for the year. If you're bored with where you live and want some action, Lipps, Inc. will show you where to go. "Won't you take me to".....
   A MacArthur Park
   B Xanadu
   C Key Largo
   D Funkytown   {98% correct on the Internet}

4. Whoops, we're not leaving 1980 just yet. Apparently, Captain and Tennille used this song as part of their new image, changing from "goody-goody" to a little bit daring. It has been ranked in the top 100 rock songs of all time.....
   A Do That To Me One More Time
   B Too Hot
   C Good Girls Don't
   D Muskrat Love   {86% correct on the Internet}

5. Okay, on to 1981. This is one of those unique songs you should listen to for its interesting lyrics. It was No. 2 for the year, by Kim Carnes, and it's filled with imagery. "All the boys think she's a spy", and, even better, "She's pure as New York snow!". She's got.....
   A Bette Davis Eyes
   B Private Eyes
   C Sexy Eyes
   D Sad Eyes   {98% correct on the Internet}

6. Still 1981. This one is probably going to be pretty easy. Dolly Parton sang it. It's all about the fact that most of us have to work and put up with a lot of stuff. Yes, they just use our minds and we never get the credit.....
   A Take This Job And Shove It
   B She Works Hard For The Money
   C 9 To 5
   D Nightshift   {99% correct on the Internet}

7. One more from 1981. Popular at weddings. This Kool & The Gang song was even used to welcome the American hostages home from Iran. Party down, it's.....
   A Glory Days
   B Holiday
   C Celebration
   D (The) Hokey Pokey   {98% correct on the Internet}

8. We're skipping ahead to 1983. This song with a driving beat by Michael Sembello is about an obsessed dancer. The video showed her dancing all the time and she even gets drenched with water. She's a.....
   A Dancing Queen
   B Dancing Machine
   C Maniac
   D Goody Two Shoes   {94% correct on the Internet}

9. More 1983. This time, Eddy Grant is going to take us somewhere, in this kind of reggae-style song. It seems to be a protest song of sorts, but it's also a good dancing song. "We gonna' rock on to".....
   A Waterloo

B Montego Bay
C Sussudio
D Electric Avenue   {92% correct on the Internet}

10. On to 1984, with the No. 10 song of the year, by Ray Parker, Jr. He gives advice as to what to do if one has a problem, like if there's something strange going on in the neighborhood. "Don't get caught alone, oh, no".....
A Somebody's Watching Me
B Ghostbusters
C The Heat Is On
D King Of Pain   {92% correct on the Internet}

11. Also from 1984, this one is by Billy Ocean and is about one real fine woman. It sounds like she wears "painted-on jeans" and now she and Billy are sharing the same dream. We are talking about.....
A Sweet Caroline (Good Times Never Seemed So Good)
B Love Grows (Where My Rosemary Goes)
C Caribbean Queen (No More Love On The Run)
D Lovergirl   {92% correct on the Internet}

12. We're still in 1984. This one by Deniece Williams is nice for all the guys who aren't all that special. Her man is no Romeo, isn't rich, doesn't talk much and sings off-key. But, she loves him anyway. She wants to yell.....
A Let's Hear It For The Boy
B Stuck On You
C Crazy For You
D Head Over Heels   {97% correct on the Internet}

13. It's STILL 1984, and Tina Turner helped her comeback with this hit. In fact, it was the No. 2 song of the year. It's all about protecting oneself in a relationship. She says, "who needs a heart when a heart can be broken", in.....
A Owner Of A Lonely Heart
B Do You Really Want To Hurt Me
C What's Love Got To Do With It
D Love On The Rocks   {99% correct on the Internet}

14. Time to skip ahead to 1986. There are a few songs about addictions. Robert Palmer had the No. 27 song of the year with his. He can't sleep or eat. He says "you like to think you're immune to the stuff". It's.....
   A Cocaine
   B I Want A New Drug
   C I Just Wanna Stop
   D Addicted To Love   {98% correct on the Internet}

15. Next is another 1986 hit, by Huey Lewis & The News. It was No. 13 for the year and was all about a couple staying together, even though they have been through a lot. It's.....
   A Higher Love
   B Stuck With You
   C Easy Lover
   D Stuck In The Middle With You   {84% correct on the Internet}

16. One more from 1986, and the Bangles had the No. 2 song of the year. It was unique, as the girls asked everyone to do something. We get whistling and a persistent tambourine as we try to.....
   A Walk Like An Egyptian
   B Boogaloo Down Broadway
   C Bust A Move
   D She Bop   {97% correct on the Internet}

17. Only one song from 1987. It was from Chris DeBurgh, and it was used in the soundtrack for the movie "Working Girl". It's a melancholy song and it might appeal to any guy who has a secret or unrequited love for a pretty woman.....
   A Open Your Heart
   B The Lady In Red
   C Only In My Dreams
   D La Bamba   {82% correct on the Internet}

18. It's 1988, and Billy Ocean makes a repeat appearance, with another song about a woman. In this one, he has kind of a request for the lady. He'll be her "non-stop lover", but we don't find out if she agrees.....
   A Pour Some Sugar On Me
   B Make Me Lose Control
   C Catch Me (I'm Falling)
   D Get Outta My Dreams, Get Into My Car   {90% correct on the Internet}

19. Still 1988, and a ballad from Gloria Estefan & Miami Sound Machine. He has left her and she is so sad. She's going to pretend it doesn't hurt, but she's dying inside. She just doesn't want to say goodbye, it's.....
   A Could've Been
   B Love Bites
   C Anything For You
   D Shattered Dreams   {73% correct on the Internet}

20. We'll stay in 1988 for the big finish. You can follow the advice in this song if you just did poorly in this quiz. Or, if your rent is late or things are just not going well, Bobby McFerrin says.....
   A Don't Cry
   B Don't Let The Sun Catch You Crying
   C Don't Worry Be Happy
   D Don't You Worry 'Bout A Thing   {98% correct on the Internet}

GAME 3 - MATCH THE LYRICS WITH THE 80s SONG

If you paid attention to 80s lyrics, you should do okay on this one.

1. "...nothing had the chance to be good...I'll keep holding on..."
   A All Out Of Love by Air Supply
   B Point Of No Return by Expose
   C Trouble by Lindsey Buckingham
   D Holding Back The Years by Simply Red   {66% correct on the Internet}

2. "...I want to....squeeze you, please you, I just can't get enough..."
   A Lovin' Every Minute Of It by Loverboy
   B Rapture by Blondie
   C I'm So Excited by the Pointer Sisters
   D Everybody Have Fun Tonight by Wang Chung   {82% correct on the Internet}

3. "Super highways....behind the wheel....across the nation....got to have a celebration!"
   A Living In America by James Brown
   B Celebration by Kool and the Gang
   C Freedom by Wham!
   D Vacation by Go-Go's   {49% correct on the Internet}

4. "....the fire starts to mellow....the pages start to yellow....I'll be in love with you."
   A Living Years by Mike and the Mechanics
   B Longest Time by Billy Joel
   C Through The Years by Kenny Rogers
   D Longer by Dan Fogelberg
   E Endless Love by Diana Ross and Lionel Richie   {53% correct on the Internet}

5. "You're the poet in my heart"
   A Express Yourself by Madonna
   B Poetry Man by Phoebe Snow
   C Gypsy by Fleetwood Mac

D Sara by Fleetwood Mac
   E Sara Smile by Daryl Hall and John Oates   {48% correct on the Internet}

6. "We danced until the night became a brand new day...."
   A At This Moment by Billy Vera and the Beaters
   B Longest Time by Billy Joel
   C September Morn by Neil Diamond
   D One Moment In Time by Whitney Houston   {70% correct on the Internet}

7. "...it helps to think we might be wishing on the same bright star..."
   A Eye In The Sky by Alan Parsons Project
   B Somewhere Out There by Linda Ronstadt and James Ingram
   C Heaven by Bryan Adams
   D Up Where We Belong by Joe Cocker and Jennifer Warnes
                                      {82% correct on the Internet}

8. "...I'm glad they came along, I dedicate this song..."
   A Every Woman In The World by Air Supply
   B Friends And Lovers by Gloria Loring and Carl Anderson
   C To All The Girls I've Loved Before by Julio Iglesias and Willie Nelson
   D Naughty Girls by Samantha Fox
   E Bad Girls by Donna Summer   {89% correct on the Internet}

9. "Sleight of hand and twist of fate, on a bed of nails she makes me wait..."
   A With Or Without You by U2
   B Mad About You by Belinda Carlisle
   C Missing You by John Waite
   D Stuck With You by Huey Lewis and the News   {79% correct on the Internet}

10. ."...you're every breath that I take....every step I make....two hearts that beat as one...."
   A Glory Of Love by Peter Cetera
   B Greatest Love Of All by Whitney Houston
   C Higher Love by Steve Winwood

   D Endless Love by Diana Ross and Lionel Richie   {72% correct on the Internet}

11. "...don't play games with my affection....don't leave me with no direction...."
   A Say Say Say by Paul McCartney and Michael Jackson
   B Miss You Like Crazy by Natalie Cole
   C Miss You Much by Janet Jackson
   D Talk To Me by Stevie Nicks   {42% correct on the Internet}

12. "Dig if u will the picture of u and I engaged in a kiss...."
   A I'm On Fire by Bruce Springsteen
   B Keep The Fire Burnin' by REO Speedwagon
   C Back To Life by Soul II Soul
   D When Doves Cry by Prince
   E Need You Tonight by INXS   {78% correct on the Internet}

13. "…teacher, leave those kids alone…"
   A Church Of The Poison Mind by Culture Club
   B Off The Wall by Michael Jackson
   C Trouble by Lindsey Buckingham
   D Another Brick In The Wall by Pink Floyd   {95% correct on the Internet}

14. "...live together in perfect harmony, side by side on my piano keyboard…"
   A Crimson And Clover by Joan Jett
   B Friends And Lovers by Gloria Loring and Carl Anderson
   C You And I by Eddie Rabbitt and Crystal Gayle
   D Ebony And Ivory by Paul McCartney and Stevie Wonder
                                              {88% correct on the Internet}

15. "Don't wanna see your face, you better disappear. The fire's in their eyes...."
   A Bust A Move by Young MC
   B Let It Whip by Dazz Band
   C Roll With It by Steve Winwood
   D Beat It by Michael Jackson   {68% correct on the Internet}

16. "Life is a moment in space, when the dream is gone it's a lonelier place…"
   A Woman In Love by Barbra Streisand
   B Every Woman In The World by Air Supply
   C Greatest Love Of All by Whitney Houston
   D She's Like The Wind by Patrick Swayze and Wendy Fraser
   {56% correct on the Internet}

17. "…She's the one, the one for me….the kind of girl that makes you feel nice…."
   A Carrie by Europe
   B Joanna by Kool and the Gang
   C Gloria by Laura Branigan
   D Rosanna by Toto   {65% correct on the Internet}

18. "There'll be some sweet sounds comin' down…."
   A All Those Years Ago by George Harrison
   B Glory Days by Bruce Springsteen
   C Nightshift by the Commodores
   D One Moment In Time by Whitney Houston   {71% correct on the Internet}

19. "….I've been waiting…. I've been waiting…. I've been waiting….Yeah, waiting…."
   A All Cried Out by Lisa Lisa and Cult Jam
   B All Out Of Love by Air Supply
   C Waiting For A Girl Like You by Foreigner
   D Missing You by John Waite
   E Wasted On The Way by Crosby, Stills and Nash   {76% correct on the Internet}

20. "…It shakes all over like a jelly fish…I kinda like it…"
   A Real Love by Jody Whatley
   B Crazy Little Thing Called Love by Queen
   C Neutron Dance by the Pointer Sisters
   D Stray Cat Strut by the Stray Cats   {60% correct on the Internet}

GAME 4 - WHO SANG THESE? (80s)

You'll really have to know your 80s artists for this one. (Top ten songs are in caps.)

1. THESE DREAMS; NOTHIN' AT ALL; ALONE; WHO WILL YOU RUN TO; NEVER; WHAT ABOUT LOVE.....
   A Fleetwood Mac
   B J. Geils Band
   C Little Joe & The Thrillers
   D Little River Band
   E Heart   {86% correct on the Internet}

2. TAKE IT ON THE RUN; KEEP ON LOVING YOU; CAN'T FIGHT THIS FEELING; KEEP THE FIRE BURNING; That Ain't Love; One Lonely Night.....
   A Tears For Fears
   B Reparata & The Delrons
   C REO Speedwagon
   D Eurythmics
   E U2   {95% correct on the Internet}

3. HARD TO SAY I'M SORRY; HARD HABIT TO BREAK; YOU'RE THE INSPIRATION; WILL YOU STILL LOVE ME?; LOOK AWAY; YOU'RE NOT ALONE.....
   A Air Supply
   B Chicago
   C Boston
   D Sacramento
   E Eagles   {86% correct on the Internet}

4. PLEASE DON'T GO GIRL; HANGIN' TOUGH; COVER GIRL; DIDN'T I (BLOW YOUR MIND); YOU GOT IT (THE RIGHT STUFF); I'LL BE LOVING YOU (FOREVER).....
   A New Kids On The Block
   B New Colony Six
   C New Edition
   D New Order
   E Huey Lewis & The News   {81% correct on the Internet}

5. HE'S SO SHY; SLOW HAND; AUTOMATIC; I'M SO EXCITED; JUMP (FOR MY LOVE); NEUTRON DANCE.....
   A Dexys Midnight Runners
   B Supertramp
   C Pointer Sisters
   D Joan Jett & The Blackhearts
   E Blondie   {97% correct on the Internet}

6. DE DO DO DO, DE DA DA DA; DON'T STAND SO CLOSE TO ME; EVERY LITTLE THING SHE DOES IS MAGIC; KING OF PAIN; WRAPPED AROUND YOUR FINGER; Spirits In The Material World.....
   A Journey
   B The Police
   C The Cars
   D The Police Cars
   E Duran Duran   {94% correct on the Internet}

7. LET'S GO CRAZY; I WOULD DIE 4 U; RASPBERRY BERET; POP LIFE; KISS; PURPLE RAIN.....
   A Earth, Wind & Fire
   B Bobby Fleet & His Band With The Beat
   C INXS
   D Prince & The Revolution
   E Genesis   {98% correct on the Internet}

8. DO YOU REALLY WANT TO HURT ME; TIME (CLOCK OF THE HEART); I'LL TUMBLE 4 YA; CHURCH OF THE POISON MIND; KARMA CHAMELEON; MISS ME BLIND.....
   A The Cars
   B Styx
   C Cutting Crew
   D Culture Club
   E Rude Boys   {98% correct on the Internet}

9. CELEBRATION; GET DOWN ON IT; JOANNA; MISLED; FRESH; CHERISH.....
   A Kool & The Gang

B Huey Lewis & The News
  C The Romantics
  D Dicky Doo & The Dont's
  E Commodores   {94% correct on the Internet}

10. SARA; HOLD ME; BIG LOVE; LITTLE LIES; Gypsy; Everywhere.....
  A A Flock Of Seagulls
  B Starship
  C Crowded House
  D The Floaters
  E Fleetwood Mac   {64% correct on the Internet}

11. LOVERBOY; SUDDENLY; GET OUTTA MY DREAMS, GET INTO MY CAR; WHEN THE GOING GETS TOUGH, THE TOUGH GET GOING; Love Is Forever; The Color Of Love.....
  A George Michael
  B Billy Idol
  C Ike Turner
  D Billy Ocean
  E Kenny G   {91% correct on the Internet}

12. TRULY; YOU ARE; MY LOVE; ALL NIGHT LONG (ALL NIGHT); RUNNING WITH THE NIGHT; HELLO.....
  A Whitney Houston
  B Lionel Ritchie
  C Richie Petrie
  D Stevie Wonder
  E Tina Turner   {96% correct on the Internet}

13. HIT ME WITH YOUR BEST SHOT; LOVE IS A BATTLEFIELD; WE BELONG; INVINCIBLE; Fire And Ice; Little Too Late.....
  A Nervous Norvus
  B Pat Benatar
  C Chaka Khan
  D Laura Branigan
  E Stevie Nicks   {95% correct on the Internet}

14. ONE MORE NIGHT; SUSSUDIO; DON'T LOSE MY NUMBER; TAKE ME HOME; GROOVY KIND OF LOVE; TWO HEARTS.....
   A Frank Sinatra
   B Rick Astley
   C Phil Collins
   D Nathaniel Meyer
   E Richard Marx   {97% correct on the Internet}

15. UPTOWN GIRL; AN INNOCENT MAN; A MATTER OF TRUST; WE DIDN'T START THE FIRE; The Longest Time; Allentown.....
   A Billy Joel
   B Elton John
   C Michael Jackson
   D Cher
   E Sting   {99% correct on the Internet}

16. CRUMBLIN' DOWN; SMALL TOWN; LONELY OL' NIGHT; PINK HOUSES; PAPER IN FIRE; CHERRY BOMB.....
   A Cindy Lauper
   B Bryan Adams
   C Madonna
   D Otis Campbell
   E John Cougar Mellencamp   {94% correct on the Internet}

17. MAGIC; PHYSICAL; MAKE A MOVE ON ME; HEART ATTACK; XANADU; TWIST OF FATE.....
   A Irene Cara
   B Olivia Newton-John
   C Mariah Carey
   D The Singing Nun
   E Donna Summer   {97% correct on the Internet}

18. PASSION; YOUNG TURKS; INFATUATION; SOME GUYS HAVE ALL THE LUCK; LOVE TOUCH; MY HEART CAN'T TELL YOU NO.....
   A Kenny Loggins
   B Luther Vandross

C Madonna
D Sting
E Rod Stewart   {90% correct on the Internet}

19. YOU GIVE GOOD LOVE; SAVING ALL MY LOVE FOR YOU; HOW WILL I KNOW; GREATEST LOVE OF ALL; SO EMOTIONAL; WHERE DO BROKEN HEARTS GO.....
   A Tiffany
   B Lulu
   C Madonna
   D Steam
   E Whitney Houston   {96% correct on the Internet}

20. JESSIE'S GIRL; DON'T TALK TO STRANGERS; AFFAIR OF THE HEART; LOVE SOMEBODY; Human Touch; Bop 'Til You Drop.....
   A Bruce Springsteen
   B Kenny Rogers
   C Dan Steely
   D Al Stewart
   E Rick Springfield   {90% correct on the Internet}

GAME 5 - EYEING THE 80s

If you watched videos in the 80s, this quiz may be a snap for you. There is even a question that was answered correctly 100% of the time on the Internet.

1. We'll start with a song that has been listed as the number one song of the 80s and number 22 of all time! Otherwise, all you need to know is that it's 1981, and Olivia Newton John is in a health club.....
   A Private Dancer
   B Physical
   C Heart Attack
   D Shake Your Groove Thing   {97% correct on the Internet}

2. Mr. Mister had year-end top ten hits for two years in a row...Broken Wings in 1985, and this one, which at times sounds like a hymn. It seems that they want this person to follow, no matter where they go.....
   A Green-Eyed Lady
   B Kyrie
   C Little Jeannie
   D Sara   {81% correct on the Internet}

3. Editorializing.....Big Country did just great as a one-hit wonder, with this 1983 song (shades of Dexy's Midnight Runners). We hear bagpipes quite a bit and the video is kind of a "poor man's Duran Duran-type adventure".....
   A Islands In The Stream
   B Eye In The Sky
   C Ride Like The Wind
   D In A Big Country   {78% correct on the Internet}

4. It's 1987 and Madonna is now into her exotic costumes. In this video, she appears to be a "private dancer", and at the end, she dances with a little boy who couldn't get into the show (fortunately).....
   A Open Your Heart
   B Call Me
   C Lukewarm Mama
   D Centerfold   {91% correct on the Internet}

5. Kind of a strange song and video from 1983. Thomas Dolby is the artist. It's all about what a woman did to him, and it seems mostly good. "She's poetry in motion" and .....
  A She Drives Me Crazy
  B She Blinded Me With Science
  C Something Happened On The Way To Heaven
  D Ruby, Don't Take Your Love To Town   {85% correct on the Internet}

6. The next one is by good ol' Elton John, from 1984. He is missing his girl (presumably), and he is not happy. He wants to be "laughin' like children, livin' like lovers".....
  A Roll With It
  B Hurts So Bad
  C I Guess That's Why They Call It The Blues
  D Got My Mind Set On You   {97% correct on the Internet}

7. Another 1984 hit, and this time 'tis the terrific Thompson Twins, truly. (If you see the video, good luck trying to find the "twins"). Anyway, they've got a fairly simple request, so that love can start.....
  A Hold Me Now
  B Give Peace A Chance
  C Hold Me, Thrill Me, Kiss Me
  D Hold The Line   {91% correct on the Internet}

8. Songwriter Robbie Nevil made it to number 4 of 1987 with this dance number. He wrote it in a few hours and was concerned that the song didn't have much depth. Oh, well, that's the way it goes.....
  A Don't Mean Nothing
  B At This Moment
  C Faith
  D C'est La Vie   {70% correct on the Internet}

9. How about a nice depressing song? In 1982, the Motels had a hit with the same title as a Roy Orbison song. The affair is over, and she is so sad, and in the video, she is drinking big-time.....
  A Crazy Little Thing Called Love
  B Please Don't Go

   C Only The Lonely
   D Owner Of A Lonely Heart   {82% correct on the Internet}

10. Good 1984 dance song for Chaka Khan. In fact, her name is at the very beginning of the song, and is mixed into the song later, too. Other than that, she thinks she loves him. She says.....
   A I Feel For You
   B That's What Love Is For
   C Love Rollercoaster
   D One Night In Bangkok   {89% correct on the Internet}

11. This 1984 ZZ Top song is great to turn up nice and loud in the car. The video has a pretty young thing getting a make over, big-time, with the band members as guardian angels, of sorts. "She's so fine, she's all mine", she's got.....
   A Legs
   B Sexy Eyes
   C Open Arms
   D Everything Your Heart Desires   {96% correct on the Internet}

12. Big 1980 hit for Billy Joel, as high as number 5 for the year. It sounds a lot like a 50s song, with a saxaphone, even. Billy tells us, "Hot funk, cool punk, even if it's old junk".....
   A It's Your Thing
   B It's The Same Old Song
   C It's Still Rock and Roll To Me
   D It's A Miracle   {96% correct on the Internet}

13. Not a real big hit for .38 Special, but a good rock and roll song from 1982. They are really just giving some advice for those fighting the "battle of the sexes". Don't let go.....
   A Treat Her Like A Lady
   B Hold On Loosely
   C Tighten Up
   D You Can't Hurry Love   {75% correct on the Internet}

14. The Police had some big hits in the early 80s. This one is all about a student,and a teacher, whose car is "warm and dry". In the video, Sting appears to be the teacher, and the band jumps around a lot.....

A Careless Whisper
B King of Pain
C (She's) Sexy + 17
D Don't Stand So Close To Me   {89% correct on the Internet}

15. Dire Straits had the number 5 song of 1985. It was written as the result of a shopping trip to an appliance store. The video has some animated "blockheads" and the song uses the term "little faggot", which caused some problems.....
A Electric Avenue
B Money For Nothing
C Shop Around
D Take On Me   {93% correct on the Internet}

16. Madonna is getting naughty! It's the number 5 song of 1984. In the video, she's dancing on a gondola while traveling on the canals of Venice, and, she's got a lion with her. He (not the lion) makes her feel all shiny and new.....
A Like A Virgin
B Like A Rolling Stone
C Like A Prayer
D Like A Rock   {97% correct on the Internet}

17. Culture Club had four singles in the 1983 top 100. But their biggest hit was the number 4 song of 1984. In this one, the colors red, gold and green are mentioned, the video is set on an old-time riverboat, and "she comes and goes".....
A Blue Bayou
B Church Of The Poison Mind
C Karma Chameleon
D Borderline   {97% correct on the Internet}

18. Madonna again. This 1985 hit reflected the prevailing mood of the 80s. She says that "only boys that save their pennies make her rainy day". She's living in the kind of world that makes her a.....
A Freeway Of Love
B Material Girl
C Lovergirl
D Money Honey   {100% correct on the Internet}

19. This 1989 song by the Fine Young Cannibals has a really catchy beat. The video has a strange man in a striped suit, dancing quite oddly. He can't help himself, because.....
   A She Works Hard For The Money
   B She's About A Mover
   C She Drives Me Crazy
   D She Wants To Dance With Me   {90% correct on the Internet}

20. Laura Branigan had the number 7 song of 1982. This one is about a girl who seems to have problems (this can't be the Shadows of Knights' girl!). Was it the voices in her head, calling.....
   A Gloria
   B Mickey
   C Hey Paula
   D Mony, Mony   {89% correct on the Internet}

GAME 6 - MORE 80s

Some more 80s.....we hope you're enjoying it!

1. This song tells us that although it may be crazy, it's also true that you can "get caught between the moon and New York City"....
  A Arthur's Theme (Best That You Can Do) by Christopher Cross
  B Eye In The Sky by the Alan Parsons Project
  C Lost In Your Eyes by Debbie Gibson
  D Point Of No Return by Expose
  E Twilight Zone by Golden Earring   {87% correct on the Internet}

2. This is a story about a guy who met his old lover in the grocery store, and when she recognized him she spilled her purse and they laughed until they cried. Then they didn't know what to say to each other, so they got a six-pack and drank it in her car. Great communication skills.
  A Longer by Dan Fogelberg
  B One Moment In Time by Whitney Houston
  C Same Old Lang Syne by Dan Fogelberg
  D Twist Of Fate by Olivia Newton-John   {61% correct on the Internet}

3. This song has some catchy phrases: "Caught like a wildfire out of control".... "Living to run and running to live"...."Moving eight miles a minute"....
  A Against All Odds by Phil Collins
  B Against the Wind by Bob Seger & the Silver Bullet Band
  C Longest Time by Billy Joel
  D On My Own by Patti LaBalle and Michael McDonald
  E Second Chance by Thirty Eight Special   {85% correct on the Internet}

4. The singer encourages you to take your baby by the hand, or the heel, or the hair, or the ears, or the wrist -- sounds cruel! But when you're "in phase" you can do this....
  A Breakdance by Irene Cara
  B Dance Hall Days by Wang Chung

C Dancing In The Dark by Bruce Springsteen
   D Dancing In The Sheets by Shalamar
   E Dancing On The Ceiling by Lionel Richie   {61% correct on the Internet}

5. Who clowned through the video of YOU CAN CALL ME AL with Paul Simon?
   A Weird Al Yankovic
   B Steve Martin
   C Chevy Chase
   D The Mormon Tabernacle Choir   {52 correct on the Internet}

6. The artist is singing about a long-gone friend who imagined a lot and said that all he needed was love....
   A All Those Years Ago by George Harrison
   B Living Years by Mike and the Mechanics
   C Summer Of '69 by Bryan Adams
   D Through The Years by Kenny Rogers   {73% correct on the Internet}

7. This song tells of a place: not Iceland or the Philippines, but a place where the bars are temples and the gods are everywhere. A place that humbles a man....
   A Danger Zone by Kenny Loggins
   B On The Dark Side by John Cafferty
   C One Night In Bangkok by Murray Head
   D Xanadu by Olivia Newton-John   {72% correct on the Internet}

8. This guy hasn't been romanced for a while. But if you said goodbye to him tonight he would still be writing music. He doesn't care what consequences it might bring, because he has been a fool for much less....
   A All Night Long by Lionel Richie
   B Late In The Evening by Paul Simon
   C Longest Time by Billy Joel
   D Next Time I Fall by Peter Cetera with Amy Grant   {67% correct on the Internet}

9. No matter what his/her friends say, the singer tells us about his/her "frozen heart" and keeps denying that he/she feels this way:
  A Alone by Heart
  B Missing You by John Waite
  C I Guess That's Why They Call It The Blues by Elton John
  D Miss You Like Crazy by Natalie Cole
  E Miss You Much by Janet Jackson   {78% correct on the Internet}

10. This singer's parents are giving her a hard time, asking her what she's gonna do with her life. Well, her daddy's still Number 1, but when the working day is done she wants to be the one to walk in the sun. Just a-wanna....
  A Girls Just Want To Have Fun by Cyndi Lauper
  B I Love Rock 'N Roll by Joan Jett and the Blackhearts
  C On My Own by Patti LaBalle and Michael McDonald
  D Papa Don't Preach by Madonna
  E Sweetest Thing I've Ever Known by Juice Newton   {92% correct on the Internet}

11. Wait, we're having a flashback: warm nights, memories, I'm going slow, and time keeps right on moving....
  A Always by Atlantic Starr
  B At This Moment by Billy Vera and the Beaters
  C Never by Heart
  D Through The Years by Kenny Rogers
  E Time After Time by Cyndi Lauper   {73% correct on the Internet}

12. New York is everything they say, and the Sunset Strip has scantily-dressed girls. DC, San Antonio, Boston, Baton Rouge, Tulsa, Austin, Oklahoma City, Seattle, San Francisco. What can you find in all these places?
  A Dancing In The Dark by Bruce Springsteen
  B Heart Of Rock and Roll by Huey Lewis and the News
  C It's Still Rock And Roll To Me by Billy Joel
  D Nothin' But A Good Time by Poison
  E Party All The Time by Eddie Murphy   {84% correct on the Internet}

13. This guy's got a problem! He should sit down, take a look at himself: doesn't he want to be somebody? Unlucky at love, he lost his head and gambled his heart away. He was beaten by the Queen of Hearts....
   A Addicted To Love by Robert Palmer
   B The Gambler by Kenny Rogers
   C Lonesome Loser by the Little River Band
   D Owner Of A Lonely Heart by Yes
   E Two Hearts by Phil Collins   {68% correct on the Internet}

14. Some say love is a river, and some say love is a razor (what, you haven't heard anyone say that?). But what song does say that?
   A Candle In The Wind by Elton John
   B Crimson and Clover by Joan Jett
   C Every Rose Has Its Thorn by Poison
   D Sweetest Thing I've Ever Known by Juice Newton
   E The Rose by Bette Midler   {80% correct on the Internet}

15. "Auf ihrem Weg zum Horizont denkst du vielleicht...."
   A C'est La Vie by Robbie Nevil
   B Der Kommissar by After the Fire
   C 99 Luftballons by Nena
   D Take My Breath Away by Berlin
   E Xanadu by Olivia Newton-John   {66% correct on the Internet}

16. This song progresses (regresses?) from patient conversation to holding back urges to body talk to getting horizontal to animal passion. Oh, let me hear it...
   A Do That To Me One More Time by Captain and Tennille
   B Express Yourself by Madonna
   C Let's Go All The Way by Sly Fox
   D Physical by Olivia Newton-John
   E Start Me Up by the Rolling Stones   {68% correct on the Internet}

17. To Bruce: "You're like a snake in the grass...you're gonna break your glass." Well, it rhymes anyway.
   A Better Be Good To Me by Tina Turner
   B Don't Be Cruel by Bobby Brown
   C Don't Bring Me Down by the Electric Light Orchestra

   D I Can't Go For That by Hall and Oates
   E I Don't Need You by Kenny Rogers {65% correct on the Internet}

18. A quickie here: the singer wants this lady to be his "acrobat":
   A Angelia by Richard Marx
   B Billie Jean by Michael Jackson
   C Little Jeannie by Elton John
   D Nikita by Elton John
   E Sussudio by Phil Collins   {52% correct on the Internet}

19. The singer often prays that if he/she dies before he/she awakes, then could he/she make it through the night? (Remember, lyrics don't have to make sense.) Just in case, we better "cherish the life we live..."
   A Cherish by Kool and the Gang
   B More Love by Kim Carnes
   C My Love by Lionel Richie
   D Real Love by Jody Watley
   E Sweet Love by Anita Baker   {77% correct on the Internet}

20. Heavy lyrics here: all about mythical characters like Scylla and Mephistopheles....if your face is turned to alabaster, then your servant will become your master....
   A Obsession by Animotion
   B Take My Breath Away by Berlin
   C Walk Like An Egyptian by Bangles
   D Wrapped Around Your Finger by Police
   E Xanadu by Olivia Newton-John   {57% correct on the Internet}

GAME 7 - EASIN' THROUGH THE 80s

Disco's pretty much dead by now, and there are videos to help in this quiz of very popular songs.

1. This song was once listed in 158th place on the all-time list of the top rock 'n' roll songs. Hall and Oates warn us, here she comes! If you don't watch out, she'll chew you up! She's.....
   A Billie Jean
   B (The) Centerfold
   C Hungry Like The Wolf
   D (The) Maneater   {96% correct on the Internet}

2. Very memorable song and video. This helped Cyndi Lauper win the Grammy for the Best New Artist of 1984. She said that she wants to walk in the sun, and with about as much energy anyone is ever going to come up with, that.....
   A I'm So Excited
   B Girls Just Want To Have Fun
   C Somebody's Watching Me
   D I Want A New Drug   {95% correct on the Internet}

3. This song by Toto was right up there in 1982 -- like in the top 20. She's been gone for almost a year, and they didn't know that losing her would hurt so bad. Gone but not forgotten, it's.....
   A Roseanna
   B My Sharona
   C Amanda
   D Gloria   {87% correct on the Internet}

4. Just like in the 50s (and the 60s, and the 70s), the tears on their pillows bespoke the pain in their hearts in the 80s. Journey now faces reality, as "she" leaves. We never find out her name, but she is still loved. The story is.....
   A King Of Pain
   B Separate Ways (Worlds Apart)
   C Bye, Bye Love
   D Love Roller Coaster   {87% correct on the Internet}

5. Asia explained how this all happened. At first, they apparently just couldn't help themselves. Later, something went terribly wrong. They keep telling us over and over, it was the.....
  A One Night In Bangkok
  B Shadows Of The Night
  C Heat Of The Moment
  D Crazy Little Thing Called Love   {80% correct on the Internet}

6. This is not your typical love song, where it seems like lovers are either happy or one is leaving. Pat Benatar makes it quite clear that love is difficult (but they are young). Both lovers know that.....
  A You Can't Hurry Love
  B Love Is Blue
  C Love Is A Battlefield
  D Love Hurts   {90% correct on the Internet}

7. This one is just a good ol' rock 'n' roll song from 1983. Quiet Riot says they'll get wild, wild, wild. Does the singer have an evil mind.....a funny face? Girls, rock your boys, and.....
  A Cum On, Feel The Noize
  B Jump
  C Walk Like An Egyptian
  D Wake Me Up Before You Go-Go   {92% correct on the Internet}

8. Bruce Springsteen had a top 20 hit in 1984, in which he repeated several times that "this gun" was for hire. If you remember the video, he had a special dance partner at the end (a young Courtney Cox, no less). It was.....
  A Dancing In The Dark
  B Dancing Machine
  C Dance The Night Away
  D Dancing Queen   {93% correct on the Internet}

9. The next one is a nice one from Mike and the Mechanics in 1989. It's sort of a poem put to music and the video even has choir boys singing background. Say it loud, say it clear, it's.....
  A Wind Beneath My Wings
  B Like A Prayer

C Love In An Elevator
D (The) Living Years   {89% correct on the Internet}

10. High energy time again. This song is all about the Go Gos and something that they claim to have. Other than that, there's not much to it, other than doin' a dance and being in a trance. If you know the title, you know most of the lyrics.....
   A Sweet Dreams (Are Made Of This)
   B We Got The Beat
   C Pac-Man Fever
   D Open Arms   {95% correct on the Internet}

11. The Stray Cats were pretty cool cats in the 80s. (If you see the video, check out their "high" hair.) They "got cat class" and they "got cat style" in this bluesy hit from 1982. It's the.....
   A Nashville Cats
   B Stray Cat Strut
   C Alley Cat
   D Year Of The Cat   {89% correct on the Internet}

12. Bananarama hit it big in 1987 with a great dancing song about an ex-boyfriend who may have a broken heart. The question is do they give this guy a second chance. They seem to be happy (smug?), when they say.....
   A Control
   B Another One Bites The Dust
   C I Heard A Rumor
   D Footloose   {80% correct on the Internet}

13. Wait a minute.....who's singing this song and what's the title? I get confused. Oh, yeah, it's the Pet Shop Boys singing about a West End town with dead-end walls and some of the people who live there. It's.....
   A West End Girls
   B California Girls
   C Girls, Girls, Girls
   D Bennie And The Jets   {95% correct on the Internet}

14. This was a top ten song in 1983 for U.K. artist and husky-throated Bonnie Tyler. She seemed to be having love troubles (maybe you can figure out what the song means). It's clear she wants to spend the night with this guy, though. It's.....
   A She Works Hard For The Money
   B 99 Luft Balloons
   C Total Eclipse Of The Heart
   D Promises, Promises   {93% correct on the Internet}

15. Big song, big video in '83 for "pretty boys" Duran Duran. He's on the hunt, he's after her, alright. The song is all about the chase, and the video was set mostly in the jungle. The song is.....
   A Eye Of The Tiger
   B Bungle In The Jungle
   C See You Later, Alligator
   D Hungry Like The Wolf   {90% correct on the Internet}

16. This 1983 Men at Work song bested their 1982 hit "Who Can It Be Now". A flute is heard often and we hear about vegemite sandwiches. "You better run, you better take cover", it's.....
   A Africa
   B Key Largo
   C Islands In The Stream
   D Down Under   {94% correct on the Internet}

17. The Police did alright for themselves. This one should be easy -- Sting and the boys had the No. 1 song of 1983. Is it a love song, or is it darker.....something about jealousy and obsession? It's.....
   A Waiting For A Girl Like You
   B Every Breath You Take
   C Eye In The Sky
   D Hungry Eyes   {93% correct on the Internet}

18. Way to go Dexy's Midnight Runners! This song starts with a reference to "poor old Johnny Ray". The video is just a little bit unique. And we hear some "turra, lurras" in there. Now, she has grown, so.....
   A Come On, Eileen
   B Hello, Mary Lou

 C (She's) Sexy & 17
 D Take A Letter, Maria   {83% correct on the Internet}

19. Wait a minute! Where did we hear this song before? Oh, that was Little Eva (with her little baby sister). Kylie Minogue and HER little baby sister didn't do as well in 1988. In fact, she's in third place, after Grand Funk's version. It's.....
 A Mony, Mony
 B (The) Locomotion
 C (The) Swim
 D (The) Hokey-Pokey {96% correct on the Internet}

20. Rockwell had lots of help with this 1984 hit. His dad is Barry Gordy, Jr. and Michael Jackson wrote the song (and sang backup). Even with all this assistance, Rockwell had a problem.....
 A Burning Down The House
 B Somebody's Watching Me
 C Back On The Chain Gang
 D Love On The Rocks {77% correct on the Internet}

GAME 8 - FLASHBACKS FROM THE 80s

Remember the tune? And the lyrics? If you remember both, you should do a bang-up job.

1. Magic, spells, and mystery in the 80's: According to the singer, this "sing-ee" can have everything that might be desired. When the spell is cast, "you will get your way, when you hypnotize with your eyes..."
   A Magic by Olivia Newton-John
   B Magic by the Cars
   C You Can Do Magic by America
   D Abracadabra by the Steve Miller Band
   E Sweetest Taboo by Sade   {64% correct on the Internet}

2. Deep thoughts about "liberation and relief": the singer(s) say(s): "There is freedom within, there is freedom without". Apparently, the world is trying to build a wall between them. Hey, now.....
   A Don't Stop Believin' by Journey
   B Don't Let It End by Styx
   C Don't Talk To Strangers by Rick Springfield
   D Don't Worry Be Happy by Bobby McFerrin
   E Don't Dream It's Over by Crowded House   {79% correct on the Internet}

3. In BETTE DAVIS EYES, Kim Carnes said the teasing, "uneasing" actress was precocious and ferocious. And, she mentions another famous actress in the song. Who is it?
   A Madonna
   B Greta Garbo
   C Marilyn Monroe
   D Judy Garland
   E Mae West   {75% correct on the Internet}

4. In NIGHTSHIFT, the Commodores sang about Marvin Gaye, who "was a friend of mine." And, then they sang about another famous performer who now works the "Nightshift." Who is it?
   A Tiny Tim
   B The Big Bopper

   C Sam Cooke
   D Roy Orbison
   E Jackie Wilson   {65% correct on the Internet}

5. This catchy tune mentions Dixie, jazz, Creole, honky tonk, London town, and Guitar George:
   A Down Under by Men at Work
   B Stray Cat Strut by the Stray Cats
   C Sultans Of Swing by Dire Straits
   D Southern Cross by Crosby Stills and Nash
   E Funkytown by Lipps, Inc.   {76% correct on the Internet}

6. LIFE IN A NORTHERN TOWN, by Dream Academy, refers to which memorable year and person?
   A 1969 -- Neil Armstrong
   B 1963 -- John F. Kennedy
   C 1974 -- Richard Nixon
   D 1968 -- Martin Luther King   {55% correct on the Internet}

7. What's this all about? She wakes up, another tough morning, another day. She sings, "My ba-by works from nine till five and then....". Then, it's off to a movie, slow-dancing, anything she wants.
   A Morning Train by Sheena Easton
   B When I Think Of You by Janet Jackson
   C I Wanna Dance With Somebody by Whitney Houston
   D Nine To Five by Dolly Parton
   E Anything For You by Gloria Estefan and the Miami Sound Machine   {82% correct on the Internet}

8. A weather quiz: which one is singing of memories and new emotions? Which one wants to "talk like lovers do"...
   A It's Raining Again by Supertramp
   B Blame It On The Rain by Milli Vanilli
   C Here Comes The Rain Again by Eurythmics
   D Purple Rain by Prince
   E Mandolin Rain by Bruce Hornsby and the Range   {89% correct on the Internet}

9. And a travel quiz: "I travel the world and the seven seas -- everybody's looking for something". Then, more talk of people using and abusing.....
   A Walk Like An Egyptian by the Bangles
   B Sweet Dreams (Are Made Of This) by Eurythmics
   C Don't Talk To Strangers by Rick Springfield
   D Rapture by Blondie
   E You Give Love A Bad Name by Bon Jovi   {97% correct on the Internet}

10. Who's being sung about here? "...a girl from a "white bread world" who wouldn't go for a "backstreet guy"....
   A Gloria by Laura Branigan
   B Uptown Girl by Billy Joel
   C Dirty Diana by Michael Jackson
   D Sara by Starship
   E Sister Christian by Night Ranger   {81% correct on the Internet}

11. In the song DRIVE, The Cars ask "Who's Gonna Drive Your Car"? They also ask all of the following except one. Which one?
   A Who's gonna pick you up when you fall?
   B Who's gonna hang it up when you call?
   C Who's gonna choose the players for your team?
   D Who's gonna pay attention to your dreams?
   E Who's gonna plug their ears when you scream?   {79% correct on the Internet}

12. In EVERY BREATH YOU TAKE, the Police will be watching you. They'll also be watching for all of the following except one. Which one?
   A Every step you take
   B Every smile you fake
   C Every heart you break
   D Every claim you stake   {54% correct on the Internet}

13. Dig if u can the song title: they are engaged in a kiss...yet, they scream at each other! "This is what it sounds like..."
   A Bust A Move by Young MC
   B Purple Rain by Prince

C When Doves Cry by Prince
   D Breakout by Swing Out Sister
   E Heart And Soul by T'Pau   {83% correct on the Internet}

14. What's gonna happen as a result of all this? This song has corner-crying and rain-waiting. It's not going well, in fact..."I'm gonna swallow my tears, I'm gonna turn and leave you here..."
   A Breakout by Swing Out Sister
   B Shake It Up by the Cars
   C Shake You Down by Gregory Abbott
   D Shake Your Love by Debbie Gibson
   E Harden My Heart by Quarterflash   {81% correct on the Internet}

15. In COWARD OF THE COUNTY by Kenny Rogers, what did Tommy do to prove he wasn't a coward?
   A Made an obscene gesture to the Dillon County Sheriff after getting a parking ticket.
   B Stood up to Rio, the town bully.
   C Recorded and produced the song "Coward Of The County."
   D Took out the Gatlin Boys in the saloon.   {52% correct on the Internet}

16. A geography quiz: Who can go coast to coast by going from L.A. to Chicago? Not only that, but "Across the north and south, to Key Largo, love for sale."
   A Easy Lover by Philip Bailey, with Phil Collins
   B Smooth Operator by Sade
   C Boys Of Summer by Don Henley
   D Naughty Girls by Samantha Fox
   E West End Girls by the Pet Shop Boys   {58% correct on the Internet}

17. Who could it be? This singer is on top of the world, feeling free...."Flying away on a wing and a prayer, who could it be?"
   A (Theme from the) Greatest American Hero by Joey Scarbury
   B Pilot Of The Airwaves by Charlie Dore
   C Smooth Operator by Sade
   D Loverboy by Billy Ocean
   E Lovergirl by Teena Marie   {84% correct on the Internet}

18. In IT'S STILL ROCK 'N ROLL TO ME, either Billy Joel is living in the past or the past is part of the present. Got that? Anyway, amidst all the "hot funk, cool punk, old junk", which of these does Billy NOT suggest?
   A Maybe I should buy some old tab collars?
   B Should I get a set of white-wall tires?
   C Should I try to be a straight `A' student?
   D Can I roll my sleeve around a pack of Luckies?
   E How about a pair of pink sidewinders?   {79% correct on the Internet}

19. Haunting words and melody: Yes, they were dreamers, only dreamers. "Those summer nights when we were young, we bragged of things we'd never done."
   A Desert Moon by Dennis DeYoung
   B Captain Of Her Heart by Double
   C Dreamin' by Vanessa Williams
   D Dreaming by Cliff Richard
   E Dreaming by Orchestral Manoeuvres in the Dark   {43% correct on the Internet}

20. More haunting words and melody. According to the song, it was past midnight, and the lady still couldn't fall asleep..."too long ago, too long apart, she couldn't wait another day..."
   A Desert Moon by Dennis DeYoung
   B Captain Of Her Heart by Double
   C Dreamin' by Vanessa Williams
   D Dreaming by Cliff Richard   {35% correct on the Internet}

GAME 9 - SUBTITLES FROM THE 80s/90s

Another chance for you to show you know your subtitles. Some are fairly obvious, some are not.

1. Let's begin in late 1981 with Hall & Oates, who in the late 80s replaced the Everly Brothers as the #1 charting duo of the rock era. In this No. 1 hit they made a firm statement, I CAN'T GO FOR THAT. The subtitle.....
  A (Say It Isn't So)
  B (Must Say No)
  C (Bibbity Bobbity Boo)
  D (No Can Do)   {81% correct on the Internet}

2. Singer/songwriter John Parr had the No. 11 song of 1985 with a little number called ST. ELMO'S FIRE (from the movie of the same name). It was No. 1 for two weeks. The subtitle.....
  A (Liar, Liar)
  B (Man In Motion)
  C (I'm Smokin')
  D (Cool It Now)   {85% correct on the Internet}

3. Tag Team had one of the biggest-selling records of the rock era with their hit in 1993. The song is called WHOOMP! and the subtitle is.....
  A (Get It On)
  B (Start To Pump)
  C (There It Is)
  D (Whaz Up?)   {86% correct on the Internet}

4. In 1983, Lionel Richie, who used to be lead singer for the Commodores, had the No. 5 song which was called ALL NIGHT LONG. It had a Jamaican chant in it. Its subtitle.....
  A (Workin' At Burger King)
  B (Dancing To The Music)
  C (All Day Long)
  D (All Night)   {74% correct on the Internet}

5. In 1985, the Scottish group Simple Minds had their biggest hit and only No. 1 single with a song called DON'T YOU. This one is just begging for the right subtitle, isn't it.....
   A (Careless Whisper)
   B (Tell My Mama)
   C (Forget About Me)
   D (Won't You)   {95% correct on the Internet}

6. In 1993, Meat Loaf (born Marvin Lee Aday) had by far his biggest hit with a song called I'D DO ANYTHING FOR LOVE. It was No. 1 for 5 weeks! The rather intriguing subtitle.....
   A (But I Won't Do That)
   B (The Gentleman In Black)
   C (Except Listen To You Sing)
   D (Another One Bites The Dust)   {97% correct on the Internet}

7. In 1980, Paul McCartney & Wings had one of their biggest hits with a song called COMING UP. You get a hint (of sorts) when you learn that the studio version of the song was on the B-side. The subtitle.....
   A (Live At Glasgow)
   B (Going Down)
   C (With A Little Luck)
   D (The Ladder To The Roof)   {30% correct on the Internet}

8. How about the No. 8 song of 1991. C + C Music Factory scored big with GONNA MAKE YOU SWEAT. It had a memorable subtitle which was performed by a former weather girl who received no credit. It is.....
   A (Come And Take Me)
   B (Run Those Laps)
   C (Get Down Tonight)
   D (Everybody Dance Now)   {86% correct on the Internet}

9. Culture Club, once known as In Praise of Lemmings, had a meteoric rise in 1983. One of their biggest hits of that year was simply called TIME. It had a unique but related subtitle.....
   A (I Think She's Doing Time)
   B (Won't Bring Me Down)

C (Clock Of The Heart)
  D (Is On My Side)   {54% correct on the Internet}

10. In 1993, The Proclaimers hit it big with I'M GONNA BE, a song which people seemed to either love or hate. The subtitle.....
  A (Movin' On Down The Line)
  B (500 Miles)
  C (Eating Scones All Night)
  D (Looking For You)   {75% correct on the Internet}

11. Billy Ocean, born Leslie Sebastian Charles, had his first big hit in 1984 with CARIBBEAN QUEEN. This subtitle seems to tell a story all by itself, making Billy happy. It is.....
  A (You Are So Good Looking)
  B (We're Sharing The Same Dream)
  C (No More Love On The Run)
  D (I'll Never Let You Get Away)   {56% correct on the Internet}

12. How about that Whitney Houston.....eleven No. 1 songs since 1985! In 1987, she had the first of her three platinum singles with I WANNA DANCE WITH SOMEBODY. The subtitle.....
  A (Anybody, Even You)
  B (Who Loves Me)
  C (Do You Hear Me)
  D (Birds Fly)   {94% correct on the Internet}

13. In 1983, Journey had one of its biggest hits with SEPARATE WAYS. It was the story of two lovers breaking up and the subtitle underscores that. It is.....
  A (You Take The High Road, I'll Take The Low Road)
  B (Worlds Apart)
  C (Don't Say Goodbye)
  D (Never Will See You Again)   {72% correct on the Internet}

14. The Pointer Sisters (they really are sisters) had a memorable song in 1984, called JUMP. This was sort of a command, and the subtitle tells us why someone should be jumping. It is.....
  A (Out Of Your Skin)
  B (In The Saddle)

   C (To Show Me You Care)
   D (For My Love)   {96% correct on the Internet}

15. In 1981, Joey Scarbury had a hit that made it to No. 2 and spent 18 weeks on the charts. It was called THEME FROM THE "GREATEST AMERICAN HERO" and it was from the TV show of the same name. The subtitle.....
   A (Coming Home)
   B (Believe It Or Not)
   C (Bobby's Song)
   D (Get Out Of Town)   {82% correct on the Internet}

16. Phil Collins had his first No. 1 song in 1984, called AGAINST ALL ODDS. It was the title song from the movie. You probably know the song better by its subtitle, which is.....
   A (Do You Remember?)
   B (I'll Fight For You)
   C (Take A Look At Me Now)
   D (I'm Betting My Bottom Dollar)   {95% correct on the Internet}

17. The No. 2 hit of 1990 was BECAUSE I LOVE YOU by Stevie B. It was by far his biggest hit and spent four weeks at No. 1. It's a toughie.....
   A (The Postman Song)
   B (I'll Never Go Away)
   C (It's Alright)
   D (And It Sure Ain't Puppy Love)   {23% correct on the Internet}

18. The Eurythmics' first hit was SWEET DREAMS. It made it to No. 1 in 1983, and was on the charts for 18 weeks. It's another one that shouldn't be too tough. The subtitle.....
   A (Are Made Of This)
   B (All Night Long)
   C (The Woo Woo Song)
   D (Of The Lady In Red)   {98% correct on the Internet}

19. From 1994 we have the hit from the movie "Reality Bites". It was called STAY and was by Lisa Loeb (glasses and all) & Nine Stories. It ended up as the No. 5 song of that year. The subtitle.....
  A (I'm Ready)
  B (Never Mind, You Can Go)
  C (I Missed You)
  D (What A Feeling)   {63% correct on the Internet}

20. The last song for this game wasn't a big hit, but it's being used because it's got such a "cool" subtitle (and because we're running out of subtitle songs). It was from 1987, by Aerosmith and called DUDE. The subtitle.....
  A (Don't be Crude)
  B (Drown The Shamrock)
  C (It's Better To Be Rude)
  D (Looks Like A Lady)   {91% correct on the Internet}

GAME 10 - NAVIGATING THROUGH THE 90s

If you prefer the newer tunes, here's a game for you.

1.. We're starting with a 1994 tune by John Mellencamp and Me'Shell NegeOcello. If that didn't give it away, you should know that all the girls are dressed up for each other and the boys do the boogie-woogie on the corner. This is "calling".....
  A The Sign
  B End Of The Road
  C Wild Night
  D Joyride   {90% correct on the Internet}

2. This song by The Proclaimers was released in the late 80s, but didn't hit it big until 1993, when it was played in the movie Benny and Joon. When he wakes up, he will be waking up next to her, etc., etc., etc......
  A I'm Gonna Be (500 Miles)
  B All That She Wants
  C Can't Help Falling In Love
  D A Whole New World   {88% correct on the Internet}

3. Tom Cochrane is rockin' in this 1993 hit. He doesn't seem to be worried about very much. He even mentions Mozambique and the Khyber Pass (yes, he does). So, "just tell 'em we're survivors".....
  A Tennessee
  B Escapade
  C Life Is A Highway
  D Fantastic Voyage   {89% correct on the Internet}

4. Big hit for 10,000 Maniacs and Natalie Merchant in 1994, very orchestral. It's all about the way she feels under his command. She wants him, she wants him, she wants him; take her now, take her now, take her now.....
  A Because The Night
  B These Are Days
  C The Power Of Love
  D All I Wanna Do   {71% correct on the Internet}

5. It's the Cranberries and Dolores O'Riordan in 1994. She is head-over-heels in love. She's such a fool for him and he's got her wrapped around his finger. Can this be the same woman who sang Zombie.....
   A Whatta Man
   B Linger
   C Show Me Love
   D I Gotta Man   {72% correct on the Internet}

6. It's the 90s, so how about some alternative? Like Pearl Jam. Okay? Here we go. This one from 1993 is about teenage rebellion. "She holds the hand that holds her down. She will RISE". She's.....
   A Insane In The Brain
   B Daughter
   C Wishing On A Star
   D Walking On Broken Glass   {68% correct on the Internet}

7. In 1990, Tom Petty told us about another young girl. She was a good girl, and crazy about Elvis. But she fell into the clutches of a "bad boy" and ended up with a broken heart. Somebody, I guess Tom, was.....
   A Impulsive
   B Livin' On The Edge
   C Poison
   D Free Fallin'   {93% correct on the Internet}

8. We couldn't forget Madonna, of course. It's a ballad, from 1994. She has always been in love with him, but he took her for granted, probably because he's a "lonely star". Plus, here's a one word clue from the video.....bullfighter.....
   A Justify My Love
   B Come To My Window
   C Take A Bow
   D All For Love   {70% correct on the Internet}

9. Do you remember Right Said Fred and their muscles and bald heads, from 1992? They had one of those songs you couldn't help but notice. He's a model and he shakes his little tush on the catwalk. Any more hints from the lyrics would give it away.....
   A Rump Shaker

B Move This
  C I'm Too Sexy
  D What's Up   {94% correct on the Internet}

10. It's Metallica time. This may be tough -- it was No. 85 for 1991. It seems this young lad is having nightmares and he sleeps with one eye open. "Exit light, enter night, take my hand, off to never-neverland".....
  A Fade To Black
  B Dreaming
  C Mr. Sandman
  D Enter Sandman   {80% correct on the Internet}

11. You may not believe it, but this 1993 effort by Tag Team has been listed as the No. 1 best-selling song of the rock era. If you want to get down, they're gonna' show you the way. Shaka-laka, shaka-laka, shaka-laka, shaka-laka.....
  A Whoomp! (There It Is)
  B Baby Got Back
  C Jump Around
  D Pump Up The Jam   {78% correct on the Internet}

12. This 1991 hit by the Scorpions reflected THE Wall falling down, and all that other stuff that went with it. Okay, children of tomorrow, share your dreams, follow down to Gorky Park and listen to the.....
  A Wind Beneath My Wings
  B Voices That Care
  C Wind Of Change
  D Good Vibrations   {95% correct on the Internet}

13. It's time for another Madonna tune. This was one of her biggest hits, and was the No. 8 song of 1990. So, you're on the dance floor with a whole bunch of beautiful people, and you hear about DiMaggio and Bette Davis, among others. Strike a pose.....
  A Nothing Compares 2 U
  B Straight Up
  C Vogue
  D Express Yourself   {95% correct on the Internet}

14. In 1990, Bell Biv DeVoe had two songs in the year-end top ten....Do Me!, which was No. 10, and No. 7, a great dancing song about a very dangerous young lady. "You'll be dreamin', then screamin' demon". That girl is.....
   A Cold Hearted
   B Funkdafied
   C Dynamite
   D Poison   {79% correct on the Internet}

15. Color Me Badd had the No. 9 song of 1992. The boys were in love in this kind of bouncy, happy love song, which was considerably more discreet than their 1991 hit "I Wanna Sex You Up". And, all the things they are for her, are.....
   A More Than Words
   B Good Enough
   C All 4 Love
   D Unbelievable   {68% correct on the Internet}

16. This one was the No. 9 song of 1993, by SWV (which stands for Sisters With Voices). The girls are in love and this love really does something to them. Their hearts are "beating triple-time"! This love makes them.....
   A Weak
   B Come Undone
   C Funkdafied
   D Shine   {44% correct on the Internet}

17. This 1993 song by Arrested Development is about a homeless man who is quite special. He gives out knowledge (and gets shoes in return) and intelligent warnings about society. He's got his freedom, though. He's.....
   A Mr. Blue
   B Mr. Lonely
   C Mr. Bojangles
   D Mr. Wendal   {71% correct on the Internet}

18. In 1992, the Red Hot Chili Peppers sang a love song of sorts to a city....Los Angeles, in fact. The singer is all alone, but with the city, "together they cry". It's.....
   A Over The Rainbow
   B Up On The Roof
   C Under The Bridge
   D Over Under Sideways Down   {81% correct on the Internet}

19. In the penultimate question of this game, we'll add a footnote......this rap by Vanilla Ice was voted "the most tragic video" by MTV viewers. Somehow, it became the 22nd most popular song of 1990. Well, he does claim to be "a lyrical poet". Word to your mother, it's.....
   A Ice Ice Baby
   B Step By Step
   C Good Vibrations
   D Amazing   {98% correct on the Internet}

20. We're ending with the song which was voted "the most triumphant video" by MTV viewers. It's the 1992 Guns N' Roses hit, which was actually tragic (you figure it out). Anyway, the song and video tell the story of a marriage that ends with a suicide. Oh, well, "nothing lasts forever, even cold....."
   A Yesterday's Songs
   B November Rain
   C Lonely Days
   D Lonely Teardrops   {88% correct on the Internet}

Chapter 5 - Potpourri

GAME 1 - MEMORABLE QUOTES

Don't quote me, but I'd say there are some key lyrics here to help jog your memory. Take a run at it.....

1. "It was 20 years ago today..."
   A Ballad of the Green Berets by Sgt. Barry Sadler
   B Sgt. Pepper's Lonely Hearts Club Band by the Beatles
   C Sink the Bismarck by Johnny Horton
   D The Night Chicago Died by Paper Lace   {86% correct on the Internet}

2. "Raise the roof and have some fun.....party, karamu, fiesta, forever"
   A All Night Long by Lionel Ritchie
   B I Love Rock and Roll by Joan Jett and the Blackhearts
   C You Make Me Feel Like Dancing by Leo Sayer
   D Girls Just Want To Have Fun by Cyndi Lauper   {89% correct on the Internet}

3. "Boom shaka-laka-laka"
   A Higher Love by Steve Winwood
   B Purple Haze by Jimi Hendrix
   C Light My Fire by the Doors
   D I Want to Take You Higher by Sly and the Family Stone
                         {86% correct on the Internet}

4. "Where have you gone, Joe DiMaggio?"
   A American Pie by Don McLean
   B Reminiscing by the Little River Band
   C America by Neil Diamond
   D Mrs. Robinson by Simon and Garfunkle   {93% correct on the Internet}

5. "You know that it would be untrue, you know that I would be a liar...."
   A Higher Love by Steve Winwood
   B I Want to Take You Higher by Sly and the Family Stone
   C Purple Haze by Jimi Hendrix
   D Light My Fire by the Doors   {94% correct on the Internet}

6. "Like to tell you 'bout my baby, you know she come around...."
   A Billie Jean by Michael Jackson
   B Island Girl by Elton John
   C Judy in Disguise by John Fred and His Playboy Band
   D Gloria by the Shadows of Knight
   E Sheila by Tommy Roe   {47% correct on the Internet}

7. "Bermuda, Bahama, come on pretty mama"
   A Sea Cruise by Frankie Ford
   B Kokomo by the Beach Boys
   C Montego Bay by Bobby Bloom
   D Margaritaville by Jimmy Buffett   {96% correct on the Internet}

8. "That's me in the corner, that's me in the spotlight..."
   A Slip Slidin' Away by Paul Simon
   B Rhinestone Cowboy by Glen Campbell
   C The Joker by the Steve Miller Band
   D Losing My Religion by R.E.M.   {91% correct on the Internet}

9. "Bad...bold...wiser...hard...tough...stronger...cool...calm"
   A Feelings by Morris Albert
   B You Gotta Be by Des'ree
   C I Am..I Said by Neil Diamond
   D The Way It Is by Bruce Hornsby and the Range   {78% correct on the Internet}

10. "To everything there is a season, and a time for every purpose under heaven"
    A Turn Turn Turn by the Byrds
    B Eve of Destruction by Barry McGuire
    C Time After Time by Cyndi Lauper
    D I'm a Believer by the Monkees   {97% correct on the Internet}

11. "Drove my Chevy to the levee but the levee was dry"
    A American Pie by Don McLean
    B Time in a Bottle by Jim Croce
    C Reminiscing by the Little River Band

   D Little Deuce Coupe by the Beach Boys   {97% correct on the Internet}

12. "When the moon is in the seventh house, and Jupiter aligns with Mars..."
   A Atlantis by Donovan
   B Telstar by the Tornadoes
   C Aquarius by the Fifth Dimension
   D Rocket Man by Elton John   {92% correct on the Internet}

13. "Who you gonna call?"
   A Big Shot by Billy Joel
   B King Tut by Steve Martin
   C Mr. Big Stuff by Jean Knight
   D Superfly by Curtis Mayfield
   E Ghostbusters by Ray Parker Jr.   {99% correct on the Internet}

14. "Kinda broad at the shoulders and narrow at the hip..."
   A Mr. Big Stuff by Jean Knight
   B Big Bad John by Jimmy Dean
   C Bad Bad Leroy Brown by Jim Croce
   D Shaft (Theme from) by Isaac Hayes
   E Superfly by Curtis Mayfield   {60% correct on the Internet}

15. "Jojo left his home in Tucson, Arizona -- bought some California grass"
   A Take It Easy by the Eagles
   B New Kid in Town by the Eagles
   C Get Back by the Beatles
   D The Wanderer by Dion   {90% correct on the Internet}

16. "We don't need no education"
   A We Will Rock You by Queen
   B School's Out by Alice Cooper
   C Another Brick in the Wall by Pink Floyd
   D The Boys Are Back in Town by Thin Lizzie
   E We Gotta Get Out Of This Place by the Animals   {87% correct on the Internet}

17. "It was the 3rd of June...I was out choppin' cotton, and my brother was balin' hay"
   A Sweet Home Alabama by Lynyrd Skynyrd
   B Black Water by the Doobie Brothers
   C Tobacco Road by the Nashville Teens
   D Ode to Billie Joe by Bobbie Gentry   {67% correct on the Internet}

18. "Someone left the cake out in the rain"
   A American Pie by Don McLean
   B Dreams by Fleetwood Mac
   C MacArthur Park by Richard Harris and by Donna Summer
   D Lucy in the Sky with Diamonds by the Beatles   {79% correct on the Internet}

19. "I'm just like the guy whose feet are too big for his bed"
   A Raindrops Keep Fallin' On My Head by B.J. Thomas
   B Short People by Randy Newman
   C Ball of Confusion by the Temptations
   D I'm a Loser by the Beatles   {71% correct on the Internet}

20. "Left my home in Georgia, headed for the Frisco Bay"
   A Long Lonesome Highway by Michael Parks
   B Midnight Train To Georgia by Gladys Knight and the Pips
   C (Sittin' On) The Dock of the Bay by Otis Redding
   D Do You Know the Way To San Jose? by Dionne Warwick
   E California Dreamin' by The Mamas and the Papas   {85% correct on the Internet}

GAME 2 - SILLY SONGS

The title says it all. Have some silly fun with these....

1. Before he hit it big with the Chipmunks, David Seville had a song called WITCH DOCTOR. It was on the charts for 18 weeks and No. 1 for three. Complete the wise words of advice from the witch doctor for David's love problem. "Oo-ee-oo-ah-ah.....
   A. doobie-doobie-do"
   B. chickie-chickie-chickie-boom"
   C. ting-tang walla-walla bing-bang"
   D. whoop-whoop-whata-whata-whata" {93% correct on the Internet}

2. In 1962, Bobby "Boris" Pickett had a No. 1 called MONSTER MASH. Yes, it was a graveyard smash. This timeless tune is filled with potential trivia questions. Like, Dracula called out this question from his coffin, "whatever happened to.....
   A. my metamorphosis?"
   B. my Transylvania Twist?"
   C. my Philadelphia miss?"
   D. that neck I like to kiss?"   {86% correct on the Internet}

3. Since there are many possibilities, we will hit you with another question from MONSTER MASH Performers at the party included Igor on Chains, backed by his baying hounds. Which vocal group was about to arrive, with the Coffin Bangers.....
   A. The Dead Two Revived
   B. The Grateful Dead Alive
   C. The Lovin' Spoonful
   D. The Cryptkicker Five   {76% correct on the Internet}

4. A popular silly song from 1963 was HELLO MUDDUH, HELLO FADDUH (A LETTER FROM CAMP) by Allan Sherman. Which of these was NOT mentioned as one of the reasons for the singer's aversion to camp?
   A rain
   B critters
   C poison ivy
   D ptomaine poisoning   {61% correct on the Internet}

5. One of the masters of silly songs was Ray Stevens (born Ray Ragsdale). One of his first was the story of AHAB, THE ARAB, from 1962. This was all about the title character, and one of the things we learn is his nickname, which was.....
   A. Midnight Sandman
   B. Ol' Brown Eyes
   C. Sheik of the Burning Sands
   D. Eagle-Eye Barney   {91% correct on the Internet}

6. We are going to give you another question from AHAB, THE ARAB, too. It seems that Ahab had a camel. All you have to do is come up with the name of his camel, which was mentioned five times in the song.....
   A. Clyde
   B. Chopper
   C. Clifton
   D. Clancy   {82% correct on the Internet}

7. In 1958, Sheb Wooley had a huge hit with THE PURPLE PEOPLE EATER. It was No. 1 for six weeks that summer! This amazing creature had one eye and one horn and flew, and he sure looked strange! And we find out the reason he came here was.....
   A. to find a new friend
   B. to get a job in a rock and roll band
   C. to end the UFO mystery
   D. for lunch   {78% correct on the Internet}

8. We can manage one more from THE PURPLE PEOPLE EATER, too. Figure this one out...he ate purple people! (It is not clear if HE was purple.) But the question is...the PPE was seen on TV and he was playing rock and roll on what.....
   A. the horn in his head
   B. Elvis' guitar
   C. the ol' 88s
   D. the top of Old Smokey   {83% correct on the Internet}

9. Another master of the silly song was Roger Miller. His first and one of his biggest hits was a song called DANG ME, from 1964. It was a top-ten song and was No. 1 on the country charts for six weeks! He was the seventh of seven sons and his daddy was.....
   A. a country fool named April One
   B. a pretty darn nice guy, actually
   C. a rustler, and he'd never been outrun
   D. a pistol (and he's the son-of-a-gun)   {72% correct on the Internet}

10. Although today it wouldn't be "politically correct", the song MR. CUSTER by Larry Verne made it to No. 1 in 1960. It was a silly version of the Battle of Little Big Horn. At the beginning of the song, the "brave, young man" called out, from the rear.....
   A. "hey, I'm a skeered"
   B. "hey, let's skedaddle"
   C. "what am I doing here?"
   D. "why did you bring us here, Tonto?"   {77% correct on the Internet}

11. Brian Hyland had several hits, mostly in the 60s, but his only No. 1 was ITSY BITSY TEENIE WEENIE YELLOW POLKADOT BIKINI. She was in the locker, then came out bundled up in a blanket, then was afraid to come out of the water, where she....
   A. was drowning
   B. was turning blue
   C. was turning into a prune
   D. was sobbing and crying   {75% correct on the Internet}

12. In 1961, Lonnie Donegan And His Skiffle Group had a top-ten hit with DOES YOUR CHEWING GUM LOSE ITS FLAVOR (ON THE BEDPOST OVERNIGHT). This was a silly song, indeed! Complete this line, "if your mother says don't chew it.....
   A. do you swallow it in spite?"
   B. do you keep it out of sight?"
   C. does it make you want to fight?"
   D. do you take just one last bite?"   {66% correct on the Internet}

13. If you are old enough, you must remember Tiny Tim (born Herbert Khaury) and his unique 1968 remake called TIP-TOE THRU' THE TULIPS WITH ME. At the very beginning of the song, he sings that she should tip-toe where, which is where he'll be.....
  A. by the seashore
  B. by the window
  C. by the elm tree
  D. past his girlfriend's house   {48% correct on the Internet}

14. In 1973, Jim Stafford had his biggest hit, a gold record called SPIDERS AND SNAKES. Well, Mary Lou takes him down to the swimmin' hole for...hmmmm...and he gets silly and finds what, which he shakes at her, prompting the title line.....
  A. a salamander
  B. a gopher
  C. a cow pie
  D. a frog   {52% correct on the Internet}

15. In 1958, The Playmates had a gold record with BEEP BEEP, which was about the driver of a Cadillac being followed by a car 1/3 the Cadillac's size. The guy in the little car kept tooting his horn. The tempo got faster and faster. The little car was a...
  A. Nash Rambler
  B. VW Beetle
  C. Yugo
  D. Fiat sedan   {58% correct on the Internet}

16. One of the best parodies of all time was LEADER OF THE LAUNDROMAT, by The Detergents, released in 1964. It made fun of the song Leader of the Pack by The Shangri-Las. In this tune, what were the names of the loving couple.....
  A. Ralph and Alice
  B. Barney and Thelma Lou
  C. Freddy and Millie
  D. Murray and Betty   {20% correct on the Internet}

17. Another "politically incorrect" silly song, which probably wouldn't be released today is THEY'RE COMING TO TAKE ME AWAY, HA-HAAA!, from 1966. It made it to No. 3, but was only on the charts for five weeks! We rarely do this, but name the artist.....
   A. Nervous Norvus
   B. Bibbity Bob And The Bing Bongs
   C. Napoleon XIV
   D. Ready Freddy   {30% correct on the Internet}

18. Chuck Berry had many influential records, but MY DING-A-LING, from 1972 was his only No. 1 (how did that happen?). In the beginning of the song we get a description of his ding-a-ling, silver bells hanging on a string, which was given to him by.....
   A. Santa Claus
   B. his baby-sitter
   C. his grandmother
   D. no one...he found it   {41% correct on the Internet}

19. In 1958, a group called The Silhouettes made it to No. 1 with GET A JOB. This gold record was also a No. 1 R&B hit for six weeks. This song was filled with nonsense lyrics but they do tell us one thing about the job. It was a job.....
   A. that he said "take this job and shove it"
   B. that he didn't want anyway
   C. that he never could find
   D. that he prayed for   {46% correct on the Internet}

20. Last question is about the top ten hit from 1968 called HERE COMES THE JUDGE, by a one-hit wonder named Shorty Long. The court's in session.....you need to name the TV show with a recurring gag that inspired this song.....
   A. Ironside
   B. Rowan & Martin's Laugh-In
   C. The Dean Martin Show
   D. The Carol Burnett Comedy Hour   {72% correct on the Internet}

GAME 3 - PRETITLES THROUGH THE YEARS

Lots of songs have subtitles, but not so many have "pretitles". This game should be relatively simple (until you get to the last few).

1. First is ROCK AROUND THE CLOCK, by Bill Haley And His Comets. This song was No. 1 for eight weeks in 1955 and was featured in the movie "Blackboard Jungle". Its pretitle.....
   A (Let's All)
   B (Roll And)
   C (We're Gonna)   {93% correct on the Internet}

2. Next in line is another 50s smash, called TEDDY BEAR, by the King himself, Elvis Presley. In 1957, this song was No. 1 for seven weeks! I guess songs really had staying power back then. The pretitle.....
   A (Hold Me, I'm Your)
   B (Let Me Be Your)
   C (I'm Just A Stuffed)   {96% correct on the Internet}

3. Hold on to your coffee, as we zoom ahead all the way to 1991 and a pretitle which shouldn't be too tough. We have Bryan Adams and a song called I DO IT FOR YOU. It was featured in the movie "Robin Hood, Prince of Thieves". The answer.....
   A (Yabba Dabba Doo)
   B (Whatever You Want)
   C (Everything I Do)   {97% correct on the Internet}

4. Two giant steps back will take us to 1978 and the late Andy Gibb, with THICKER THAN WATER. This song was No. 1 for two weeks and made it to gold record status. Its pretitle.....
   A (Love Is)
   B (Your Head Is)
   C (We Are)   {97% correct on the Internet}

5. Once listed as the No. 200 song of all-time, John Lennon recorded STARTING OVER in 1980. Released just before his death, this song was No. 1 for five weeks. Its pretitle.....
   A (The Beatles Won't Be)
   B (Just Like)
   C (Happy That We're)   {93% correct on the Internet}

6. Another very highly rated pretitle song was CLOSE TO YOU, by The Carpenters. Unfortunately, Karen Carpenter is no longer with us. This was the duo's first hit and it was No. 1 for four weeks in 1970. The title began with.....
   A (They Long To Be)
   B (Up On The Roof And)
   C (Let Me Get)   {86% correct on the Internet}

7. Coincidentally, the next most popular pretitle song was also performed by an artist who met an untimely demise. This refers to Otis Redding and THE DOCK OF THE BAY, recorded three days before his death in 1967. The pretitle is.....
   A (Sittin' On)
   B (Fishin' From)
   C (Gazing Off)   {98% correct on the Internet}

8. Fortunately, this sad list does not continue. In 1976, KC And The Sunshine Band made it to No. 1 with a song called SHAKE YOUR BOOTY. It was also a big hit on the R&B charts. Its pretitle.....
   A (C'mon Everybody And)
   B (Salt And Pepper)
   C (Shake, Shake, Shake)   {92% correct on the Internet}

9. In 1977, Rita Coolidge had her first and biggest hit with a song called HIGHER AND HIGHER. A gold record, this song was a big hit while Rita was married to Kris Kristofferson (just "for the record"). Its pretitle.....
   A (I Want You To Take Me)
   B (Your Love Has Lifted Me)
   C (Let's Get Down Then Go)   {89% correct on the Internet}

10. Well, how about slipping back in to the 60s, for a Rolling Stones hit from 1965. SATISFACTION is certainly one of the most memorable oldies and probably one of the most played. The title begins with.....
  A (What I Want Is)
  B (Honey Give Me Some)
  C (I Can't Get No)   {99% correct on the Internet}

11. In 1987, Bill Medley (of the Righteous Brothers) and Jennifer Warnes (lead in the L.A. production of Hair) had a big hit with THE TIME OF MY LIFE. This song was featured in the movie "Dirty Dancing". Its pretitle is.....
  A (Right Now Is)
  B (9:00 P.M. Is)
  C (I've Had)   {93% correct on the Internet}

12. In 1975, B.J. Thomas hit No.1 with ANOTHER SOMEBODY DONE SOMEBODY WRONG SONG, which was also No. 1 on the Country and Adult Contemporary charts. The title began.....
  A (Hey Won't You Play)
  B (Turn It Up It's)
  C (Mr. DJ Let's Hear)   {92% correct on the Internet}

13. This next one may be a toughie, but maybe not. In 1990, the duo called Nelson had a gold record with LOVE AND AFFECTION. You may know that these are the twin sons of the late Ricky Nelson. This song title began with.....
  A (Baby, I Need)
  B (Can't Live Without Your)
  C (Peace)   {74% correct on the Internet}

14. We mentioned the Righteous Brothers earlier, and in 1966, they had a gold record called SOUL AND INSPIRATION. This song by baritone Bill Medley and tenor Bobby Hatfield had a pretitle which was.....
  A (Lord, It's Just)
  B (You're My)
  C (Hearts On Fire)   {96% correct on the Internet}

15. In 1972, Luther Ingram had a hit with I DON'T WANT TO BE RIGHT. This song made it to No. 3 and was an R&B No. 1 for four weeks. Its pretitle was almost as long as the main title.....
  A (You Tell Me It's Wrong, But)
  B (If Loving You Is Wrong)
  C (Right Right, You Know)   {96% correct on the Internet}

16. Paul Anka hadn't had a big hit in almost fifteen years when he made it to No. 1 in 1974 with a song called HAVING MY BABY. We seem to recall that this was criticized as a sexist song, but without getting involved in that, pick the short pretitle.....
  A (You're)
  B (Mary's)
  C (Without)   {91% correct on the Internet}

17. We are moving to 1987 for a song by Cutting Crew called DIED IN YOUR ARMS. This was the first and biggest hit for this British group. Its pretitle.....
  A (He Told Me He)
  B (My Love)
  C (I Just)   {91% correct on the Internet}

18. You may not be too familiar with this next song from 1977, but it was a gold record and made it to No.4 (No. 1 on the R&B charts). It was by a group called L.T.D. and was called BACK IN LOVE AGAIN. Its pretitle.....
  A (Every Time I Turn Around)
  B (Baby, Don't You Know)
  C (It's True, It's True, I'm)   {45% correct on the Internet}

19. As we near the end of the quiz, we return to the King, back in 1959. That year, Elvis had one of his many super hits with a song called A FOOL SUCH AS I. Previously a country hit in 1953, its title began with.....
  A (You Know That There's Never Been)
  B (Shame On Me)
  C (Now and Then There's)   {44% correct on the Internet}

20. For the last song, we have to go to 1968 for a gold record by Aretha Franklin called SINCE YOU'VE BEEN GONE. This was one of the many hits for a lady whose success has spanned four decades. The song's pretitle.....
  A (Sweet Sweet Baby)
  B (Never Feeling Right)
  C (Can I Get A Witness)   {41% correct on the Internet}

GAME 4 - ONE-HIT WONDERS

All of these questions have to do with performers that hit it big just once. The fact that they are one-hit wonders may help you....or will it?

1. Big sixties tune from a one-hit wonder with ties to the Temptations, the Marvelettes, and Jackie Wilson. The song proclaimed: "I can Mash Potato, I can do the Twist -- watch me now!"
   A Do You Want To Dance by Bobby Freeman
   B Do You Love Me by the Contours
   C Dancing In The Street by Martha and the Vandellas
   D Peppermint Twist by Joey Dee and the Starliters   {86% correct on the Internet}

2. A sixties one-hit wonder who sings "when I look into your big brown eyes, it's so very plain to see"....
   A The Rain, The Park And Other Things by the Cowsills
   B The Birds And The Bees by Jewel Akens
   C Everlasting Love by Carl Carlton
   D Puff The Magic Dragon by Peter Paul and Mary   {92% correct on the Internet}

3. Early seventies one-der from a group formed in high school. They tempted the ladies: "I'm a friendly stranger in a black sedan...I'll take you to the nearest star..."
   A Express by B. T. Express
   B Hot Rod Lincoln by Commander Cody
   C Vehicle by the Ides of March
   D Drive by the Cars   {70% correct on the Internet}

4. The 1-shot instrumental hit that was NOT the theme song from a movie:
   A Gonna Fly Now by Bill Conti
   B Chariots Of Fire by Vangelis
   C The Good, The Bad, And The Ugly by Hugh Montenegro
   D Stranger On The Shore by Acker Bilk
   E The Entertainer by Marvin Hamlisch   {81% correct on the Internet}

5. The one-hit group whose song had the same name. The group was formed by Don Grady (Robbie Douglas of "My Three Sons").
   A Yellow Balloon (1967)
   B Hot Butter (1972)
   C T. Rex (1972)
   D Flying Machine (1969)   {47% correct on the Internet}

6. The one-hit-only 1962 song that asked for the "biggest lecture" the singer ever had. She wants "a brave man", she wants "a cave man"...
   A Stormy by the Classics IV
   B Johnny Get Angry by Joanie Sommers
   C Fool (If You Think It's Over) by Chris Rea
   D Mr. Lee by the Bobbettes
   E Leader Of The Pack by the Shangri-Las   {63% correct on the Internet}

7. An 80's 1-hit wonder (all the rest were 50's 1-hit wonders):
   A Band Of Gold by Don Cherry
   B Little Star by the Elegants
   C Pink Shoe Laces by Dodie Stevens
   D Nel Blu Dipinto Di Blu by Domenico Modugno
   E Tainted Love by Soft Cell   {90% correct on the Internet}

8. The one-hitter that sang about somewhere -- where the "days are short and the nights are long":
   A California Sun by the Rivieras
   B Desert Moon by Dennis DeYoung
   C Seasons In The Sun by Terry Jacks
   D Wild Weekend by the Rebels   {58% correct on the Internet}

9. What you need, according to this one-timer, when you're all broken up because you've lost your girl...in other words, "when you're in a mess and you feel like cryin'":
   A Something So Strong by Crowded House
   B Everlasting Love by Carl Carlton
   C Little Bit Of Soul by the Music Explosion

D Different Drum by the Stone Poneys
  E Smile A Little Smile For Me by Flying Machine   {58% correct on the Internet}

10. All one-hit one-ders related to a TV show except for one. Which is it?
  A Here Comes The Judge by Shorty Long
  B Happy Days by Pratt and McClain
  C Welcome Back by John Sebastian
  D The Curly Shuffle by Jump 'n the Saddle
  E The Jerk by the Larks   {70% correct on the Internet}

11. Which sixties one-timer sang: "One day you're up and the next day you're down". And, they remind us that the grass is always greener on the other side....
  A Na Na Hey Hey Kiss Him Goodbye by Steam
  B We Ain't Got Nothin' Yet by the Blues Magoos
  C All Right Now by Free
  D I'm Down by the Beatles   {54% correct on the Internet}

12. A bouncy old one-der, this one: "Old man rhythm is in my shoes, it's no use sittin' and singin' the blues..."
  A Keep On Dancing by the Gentrys
  B Dancing In The Street by Martha and the Vandellas
  C Sea Of Love by Phil Phillips
  D Sea Cruise by Frankie Ford
  E I Got Rhythm by the Happenings   {57% correct on the Internet}

13. The one big hit for the individual or group that sang about long-haired hippies who need not apply for a job, but who thank the Lord anyway with the proclamation "I'm alive and doin' fine!"
  A Signs by the Five Man Electrical Band
  B I'm Easy by Keith Carradine
  C Get Together by the Youngbloods
  D Don't Give Up On Us by David Soul
  E Get A Job by the Silhouettes   {88% correct on the Internet}

14. A one-hit wonder-ful set of lyrics here: "When the weather's fine, you got women, you got women on your mind..."
　A　Summer Song by Chad and Jeremy
　B　Summertime by Billy Stewart
　C　In The Summertime by Mungo Jerry
　D　California Sun by the Rivieras　　　{81% correct on the Internet}

15. Which one of these one-hit wonders was a direct take-off from a number 1 hit by the Shangri-Las?
　A　Snoopy Vs. The Red Baron by the Royal Guardsmen
　B　Purple People Eater by Sheb Wooley
　C　Disco Duck by Rick Dees and His Cast of Idiots
　D　Leader Of The Laundromat by the Detergents
　E　Pac-Man Fever by Buckner and Garcia　　　{85% correct on the Internet}

16. The show business people: which was NOT a one-hit wonder (he/she/they had NUMEROUS top ten hits!)
　A　This Diamond Ring by Gary Lewis and the Playboys
　B　Rock-A-Bye Your Baby With A Dixie Melody by Jerry Lewis
　C　King Tut by Steve Martin
　D　Respect Yourself by Bruce Willis
　E　McArthur Park by Richard Harris　　{76% correct on the Internet}

17. Which of these historically-minded songs/ballads was NOT done by a one-hit wonder? In fact, the singer(s) had 3 top-ten "history hits" around 1960.
　A　Keem-O-Sabe by Electric Indian
　B　Mr. Custer by Larry Verne
　C　The Battle Of New Orleans by Johnny Horton
　D　Tobacco Road by the Nashville Teens
　E　The Night Chicago Died by Paper Lace　　　{84% correct on the Internet}

18. This one-hit wonder told of something that "stood and watched" as his baby left town..."you could have done something, but you didn't try..."
   A Alley Cat by Bent Fabric
   B Desert Moon by Dennis DeYoung
   C Mockingbird by Inez Foxx
   D Winchester Cathedral by the New Vaudeville Band
   E Wolverton Mountain by Claude King   {57% correct on the Internet}

19. This one-der sang ominously of the "pat on the back: beware, it just might hold you back! (Can you dig it?)"
   A Lies by the Knickerbockers
   B The Rapper by the Jaggerz
   C Signs by the Five Man Electrical Band
   D Smiling Faces Sometimes by the Undisputed Truth
   E Psychotic Reaction by Count Five   {62% correct on the Internet}

20. There's a place across the tracks, according to this one-hitter. "You take Sally, and I'll take Sue," and everyone will be rockin' through the night....
   A Hocus Pocus by Focus
   B Tobacco Road by the Nashville Teens
   C I Like It Like That by Chris Kenner
   D Funkytown by Lipps, Inc.
   E Yellow Balloon by Yellow Balloon {58% correct on the Internet}

GAME 5 - JAMMIN' WITH THE JACKSONS

Do your kids know that Michael first hit it big all the way back in 1969? Seems so long ago....

1. This one basically started it all in late 1969. People didn't know who was singing. Was it Diana Ross, maybe? The song was originally meant to be recorded by Gladys Knight and the Pips.....
    A Little Bitty Pretty One
    B I Want You Back
    C Sugar Daddy
    D ABC   {42% correct on the Internet}

2. Skipping all the way to 1991, and Michael is looking different now. This one is about how we are all pretty much the same. He dances with Native Americans in the video, which also contains the famous "morphing" sequence.....
    A Man In The Mirror
    B Human Nature
    C Black Cat
    D Black And White   {82% correct on the Internet}

3. Big song for Michael, early 1980, and listed as high as No. 3 for that year. It was a mellow dance number and the video had Michael in a very sparkly suit. He wants to "dance the night away".....
    A Steppin' Out
    B Never Can Say Goodbye
    C Tiny Bubbles
    D Rock With You   {80% correct on the Internet}

4. In early 1990, Janet Jackson wanted to take us (or someone) on a trip of sorts. This song made it to No. 1. One of the places she wanted to go to was Minneapolis. "We'll have a good time".....
    A Escapade
    B R.O.C.K. In The U.S.A.
    C Rhythm Nation
    D Xanadu   {68% correct on the Internet}

5. The original version of this song, by Bobby Day, was on the charts the day Michael was born (8/29/58). It was a big solo hit for Michael in 1972, and the setting for the song is on "Jaybird Street".....
   A Ben
   B Billie Jean
   C Rockin' Robin
   D Bird Dog   {90% correct on the Internet}

6. This was one of four top ten hits from Michael's first solo album, Off The Wall. It was kind of a disco sound, from 1979. The video has three Michaels dancing together at one point. "Touch me and I feel on fire".....
   A Don't Stop 'Til You Get Enough
   B Off The Wall
   C The Girl Is Mine
   D Shadow Dancing   {74% correct on the Internet}

7. This one, which Michael did with Paul McCartney in 1983, was No. 1 for six weeks! It is from Paul's Pipe of Peace platter, positively. The video shows them in a vaudeville act and we also see Linda and Latoya, luckily.....
   A Show You The Way To Go
   B Say, Say, Say
   C Dancing In The Street
   D P.Y.T. (Pretty Young Thing)   {88% correct on the Internet}

8. Listed as the first solo hit for Michael, in 1971, when he was thirteen. It's a nice ballad, in which he says he wants to be with his girl when she wakes up.....at the tender age of 13?! He says.....
   A The Girl Is Mine
   B My Sharona
   C Jean
   D Got To Be There   {69% correct on the Internet}

9. This was the second big hit for the Jackson Five, selling more than 2 million copies within three weeks, in 1970. It's all about how easy love can be. "Get up, girl, show me what you can do".....
   A I'll Be There
   B Dancing Machine

C ABC
D 1-2-3   {65% correct on the Internet}

10. How about a video with real L.A. gang members. This song from the Thriller album was one of three for Michael which made the 1983 top ten. Even as skinny as he is, Michael's acting very tough in this one, in his red jacket.....
A Beat It
B Wanna Be Startin' Somethin'
C Dirty Diana
D Nasty   {96% correct on the Internet}

11. This Jackson Five song was No. 1 for five weeks in 1970. It was redone by Mariah Carey in 1992, and she was pretty successful, too. It's sort of "Stand By Me" in reverse. Just call his name and.....
A Let's Get Serious
B I'll Be There
C I Wanna Be Where You Are
D I'll Take You There   {98% correct on the Internet}

12. Another big Jackson Five hit, and it's the last one using that name. It also seems to foreshadow the future, although the song was about a girl, not Michael. She's "automatic, systematic" and "super bad".....
A Dancing Machine
B Shake Your Body (Down To The Ground)
C Dynamite
D Venus   {62% correct on the Internet}

13. Janet is not very happy in this 1986 song and video production, which is set in a malt shop. She basically keeps saying the same thing over and over, and ends up dumping her boyfriend for someone new.....
A Nasty
B Control
C What Have You Done For Me Lately
D Beat It   {81% correct on the Internet}

14. You may already know where the title of this 1972 song came from. Michael says he'll never be alone with this friend, who's always running "here and there". There are songs about muskrats, boll weevils and dead skunks, so how about a trained rat? It's
   A Mama's Pearl
   B Sugar Daddy
   C P.Y.T. (Pretty Young Thing)
   D Ben   {88% correct on the Internet}

15. This 1984 song shouldn't be too tough, mostly due to the popular video. It was directed by John Landis, had a "rap" by Vincent Price, and refers to "the funk of 40,000 years". "Something evil's lurking in the dark", it's.....
   A Dirty Diana
   B Bad
   C Black Cat
   D Thriller   {97% correct on the Internet}

16. This is another Jackson Five song which was repeated later, this time by Gloria Gaynor in 1975. It's "just another love song" by the guys. She wants to leave, or he's had enough, but he just can't do it. It's.....
   A Never Can Say Goodbye
   B Human Nature
   C Endless Love
   D Crazy Little Thing Called Love   {81% correct on the Internet}

17. A big Number1 single from the Bad album. Latoya appears in this video, too. In the video, Michael basically follows a foxy lady around a less-than-desirable neighborhood. She seems to be impressed, eventually.....
   A Dirty Diana
   B P.Y.T. (Pretty Young Thing)
   C The Girl Is Mine
   D The Way You Make Me Feel   {64% correct on the Internet}

18. Another big hit for the Jackson Five in 1970. This one is kind of a "high-energy lecture" from the boys to their nameless darling. She's been around since grade school, when they played tag. They kind of warn her.....
   A Beat It
   B Get It Together
   C The Love You Save
   D Remember The Time   {41% correct on the Internet}

19. Another big hit from the Thriller album. This song was No. 1 for seven weeks, in 1983. By this time, Michael is really getting into the dance videos. He sings something about being "careful who you love".....
   A Rockin' Robin
   B Billie Jean
   C Dirty Diana
   D P.Y.T. (Pretty Young Thing)   {92% correct on the Internet}

20. The last one for this game is the most recent of the songs. It is from 1992, and since Michael can play a real bad dude in his videos, why not a basketball player? And it's with the other MJ, Michael Jordan, no less. It's.....
   A Jam
   B Man In The Mirror
   C Bad
   D Basketball Jones   {74% correct on the Internet}

GAME 6 - THE BRITISH INVASION

There's so much material from this segment that we were pretty much able to skip the Beatles.

1. We are starting with a few hits from The Hollies, who were very popular in the late 60s and early 70s. Their first big hit was called BUS STOP. When the singer first met his bride-to-be at the title location, what did he ask her to share.....?
   A his lunch
   B his love
   C his umbrella
   D her bus fare   {92% correct on the Internet}

2. Graham Nash, later of Crosby, Stills and Nash (and Young) was a guitarist and singer for the Hollies, whose next top-ten hit was called STOP, STOP, STOP, from late 1966. In this song, the obsessed singer desperately wanted who or what to "stop".....?
   A Lady Godiva
   B a belly dancer
   C his auto
   D his girlfriend   {40% correct on the Internet}

3. The Hollies had their last top-ten hit of the 60s with a song called CARRIE-ANNE, which had a unique steel drum interlude. In the beginning of the song, the singer said that when they were at school, Carrie-Anne "played the monitor" and he "played the....."?
   A janitor
   B steel drum
   C principal
   D doctor   {70% correct on the Internet}

4. The next British invasion group we'll "trivialize" is The Animals, who had their first and biggest hit in 1964 with THE HOUSE OF THE RISING SUN. Is it too easy if we ask where the house was? Well.....?
   A Tokyo
   B Kansas City
   C Montpelier
   D New Orleans   {94% correct on the Internet}

5. In 1965, the Animals, featuring the vocals of Eric Burdon, did pretty well with a song called WE GOTTA GET OUT OF THIS PLACE. In this song, the singer mentions his daddy. Where and/or what was his daddy doing.....?
   A leaving town again
   B he was in bed, a-dyin'
   C visiting Paris
   D drinking all night   {59% correct on the Internet}

6. One of the most prolific groups of the British invasion was The Dave Clark Five, from Tottenham, England. One of their first big hits was DO YOU LOVE ME, which was a cover version of which group's 1962 hit.....?
   A Reparata and the Delrons
   B The Orlons
   C The Contours
   D The Silver Beatles   {81% correct on the Internet}

7. The Dave Clark Five songs were mostly beat-driven and very up-tempo. In 1964, they showed their "other side" with their first slow song, which was almost not released, but became one of their biggest hits. The title.....?
   A Because
   B Bits and Pieces
   C Can't You See That She's Mine
   D Reelin' And Rockin'   {52% correct on the Internet}

8. In late 1964, the Dave Clark Five released a song called ANY WAY YOU WANT IT, showing themselves to be quite an agreeable lot. The phrase used as the refrain was repeated 28 times in the song, in four intervals at sevens time each. It was.....?
   A "that's just ok"
   B "boogety, boogety, boogety, shoo"
   C "she's not there"
   D "it's alright"   {82% correct on the Internet}

9. In 1965, Dave and the boys made it to No. 4 with a song called CATCH US IF YOU CAN, which was from their movie with the same name (in the U.K.). However, in the U.S., the movie was released under a different title, which was.....?
   A Magical Mystery Tour
   B Putney Swope
   C Having A Wild Weekend
   D I Like It Like That   {51% correct on the Internet}

10. In late 1965, the DC5 had what is listed as their only No. 1 hit, called OVER AND OVER. To answer this question correctly, all you have to do is to pick out what the singer said, "over and over again".....
   A "there's no place like home"
   B "this dance is gonna' be a drag"
   C "and I'm a believer"
   D "we're gonna' have a good time tonight"   {55% correct on the Internet}

11. Let's move on to the group many consider to be the greatest rock and roll band of all-time, The Rolling Stones. In the song SATISFACTION, where was the singer who couldn't get any satisfaction, when the "man comes on the radio".....?
   A downtown, where all the lights are bright
   B up on the roof
   C in his car
   D at the beach   {92% correct on the Internet}

12. The Stones had their fourth No. 1 hit with a song called PAINT IT BLACK, in 1966. The question is what the "Indian boy" was supposed to paint black, according to the song.....?
   A a "blue heart"
   B his face
   C a red door
   D a gold chain   {64% correct on the Internet}

13. The Stones had their next No. 1 with a song called RUBY TUESDAY, from early 1967. In this haunting tune, we learn about the mysterious title character. What does the song say about where Ruby was from.....?

A she was born in New Orleans
B she lived in dark and dirty Soho
C she was born in London at a very early age
D she would never say where she came from   {80% correct on the Internet}

14. In 1964, The Zombies had their first and highest-charting hit with a song called SHE'S NOT THERE. In still another tale of love lost, we are told how she looked - "her voice was soft and cool, her eyes were....."
A pools of blue
B clear and bright
C bloodshot
D brown as autumn   {78% correct on the Internet}

15. In 1965, Wayne Fontana and the Mindbenders, from Manchester, England, had the first of their two big hits with GAME OF LOVE. According to this song, the game of love started in the Garden of Eden, when Adam said to Eve.....?
A "baby, you're for me"
B "let's get it on"
C "honey, ignore that tree"
D "sweetie, love me do"   {77% correct on the Internet}

16. Gerry And The Pacemakers came from Liverpool, England. They had three top-ten hits, one of which was FERRY CROSS THE MERSEY, from 1965. This song came from a movie starring Gerry and the boys. The name of the movie.....?
A Kung Fu Fighters From Hell
B Don't Let The Sun Catch You Crying
C Ferry Cross The Mersey
D Band On The Run   {55% correct on the Internet}

17. In 1965 and 1966, Herman's Hermits had nine consecutive top ten hits! The first one to reach No. 1 was MRS. BROWN YOU'VE GOT A LOVELY DAUGHTER. According to this song, how would this lovely girl make "a bloke feel".....?
A so proud
B like floating away

C really groovy
D far out   {70% correct on the Internet}

18. In 1965, The Yardbirds had two big hits with FOR YOUR LOVE and HEART FULL OF SOUL. This group once included one of the most famous rock guitarists of all time. The name of the guitarist.....?
A Jim Lindsey
B Glen Campbell
C Eric Clapton
D Jimi Hendrix   {92% correct on the Internet}

19. In 1965, a group from England by the name of The Silkie had their only hit with YOU'VE GOT TO HIDE YOUR LOVE AWAY. Much of the writing, music and production of this song was done by a more famous British group.....
A The Beatles
B Monty Python's Flying Circus
C The Rolling Stones
D Herman's Hermits   {82% correct on the Internet}

20. The invasion is pretty much over, it's 1968 and a group called Small Faces sang about ITCHYCOO PARK. They got high, touched the sky and repeated this musical refrain a total of 18 times.....
A "someone left the cake out in the rain"
B "nip it in the bud"
C "let it all hang out"
D "it's all too beautiful"   {73% correct on the Internet}

GAME 7 - GUYS AND GALS

People, people, people.......so many people to sing about. Here's the poop.....read the clues, figure out who it is......

1. About this young lady.....if you knew her, you would know why the singer is blue without her, his heart yearns for her, his love for her is so rare and true, and she is pretty, pretty, pretty, pretty.....
   A Sherry
   B Peggy Sue
   C Thelma Lou
   D Diana   {93% correct on the Internet}

2. Sadly, this young lady is dead. She died with her boyfriend's high school ring clutched in her hand. She was just "sweet sixteen", and lost her life when a train hit the stalled car as she somewhat foolishly retrieved the ring.....
   A Rock And Roll Rosie From Raleigh
   B Sweet Little Sixteen
   C Dream Lover
   D Teen Angel   {88% correct on the Internet}

3. Whoops, we have another dead young lady. This one lived in old shantytown, which was down by the river which flowed by the coal yards. She committed suicide and was found floating face-down in that dirty, old river.....
   A Tammy
   B Patches
   C Short Fat Fanny
   D Angel Baby   {42% correct on the Internet}

4. The next one is a lady who didn't die (whew!). This one shines with her own personal light. If she gets to know you, watch out, because she's going to own you. There really isn't any doubt, we're talking about.....
   A Kentucky Woman
   B Cherry, Cherry
   C Hilda Mae
   D Sundown   {84% correct on the Internet}

5. On to a guy who spent some time "rowing the boat ashore." And, sister helped to "trim the sails." Together now, let's all sing "Hallelujah!" He is....
   A Abraham
   B Alfie
   C Michael
   D Master Jack   {84% correct on the Internet}

6. Another guy here. We know he is away, but we don't know when he is coming back. That seems to be the key issue, and he better hurry up! Other than that, about the only other thing we know about this guy is that he is a real "sweet talker".....
   A Jimmy Mack
   B Chickie Baby
   C Nowhere Man
   D Leader Of The Pack   {81% correct on the Internet}

7. This lady is "breaking my heart" and "shaking my confidence." But even though she
treats me bad, I'm down on my knees begging her to come home.....
   A Roxanne
   B Witchy Woman
   C Evil Woman
   D Cecilia
   E Maggie May   {75% correct on the Internet}

8. This girl lives in a bad part of town and everyone puts her down, but I don't care what her daddy do, 'cause I love her. So let your hair down and tell her to Hang On.....
   A Eileen
   B Renee
   C Sloopy
   D Rhonda   {87% correct on the Internet}

9. This gal is really something else....she's thrillin', chillin', and so divine. He's been a-searchin' the whole wide world and he's finally found his...
   A Sweet Little Sixteen

B Calendar Girl
C Candy Girl
D Dungaree Doll   {52% correct on the Internet}

10. This young man feels so happy one day and the next day he feels so sad. He must learn to take the good with the bad. Each night he asks a question of the stars up above. He cries very easily (and is probably very moody). He is.....
   A Lonely Blue Boy
   B A Teenager In Love
   C Danny Boy
   D Simon Cowell   {95% correct on the Internet}

11. Back to the ladies. This one isn't very nice...she was sent from down below! She is compared to Satan and lets no one question her advice! She needs to leave and to come back no more. She is the "sweet".....
   A Hard Headed Woman
   B Donna The Prima Donna
   C Big Maude Tyler
   D Mother-In-Law   {73% correct on the Internet}

12. The next young lady planted a tree that was just a twig, was always young at heart, wrecked the car and she was sad, was surprised with a puppy one Christmas, went away in the early Spring, and was all alone when the angels came. She was.....
   A Spooky
   B Pookie
   C Honey
   D Ronnie   {73% correct on the Internet}

13. The next guy is "cool". He impresses the girls with his guitar, playing hot licks. His dad didn't dig him at all. He left for Memphis, became a star, drove a Cadillac, and got drafted. He is.....
   A The All American Boy
   B King Of The Road
   C Mr. Lee
   D Cap Huff   {55% correct on the Internet}

14. The next guy lived long ago and ate only bearcat stew! He drove a dinosaur and "knuckled" peoples' heads. He must have been cool, too, because he was "a mean motor-scooter and a bad go-getter". There he goes.....
 A Yackety Yak
 B Alley Oop
 C The Purple People Eater
 D Beasto Maristo   {80% correct on the Internet}

15. Another guy.....he was from deep down in Louisiana, living up in the woods. He could play a guitar as easy as ringing a bell, and he kept his guitar in a gunny sack. His mom told him that maybe someday, his name would be in lights. It's.....
 A Ringo
 B Johnny B. Goode
 C Jim Lindsey
 D Rebel Rouser   {99% correct on the Internet}

16. The next person is female. She sure looked good. She had big eyes, the kind that would drive one mad. And, she had full lips, which were sure to lure someone bad. She needed to be very careful, for she was.....
 A Runaround Sue
 B Ruby Tuesday
 C Lil' Red Riding Hood
 D Juanita   {75% correct on the Internet}

17. The next is a male, and not so "cool". This guy is very punctual, and is, oh, so good and kind. He is very healthy in body and mind, and is very conservative. He adores the girl next door, but his mom won't let him near her. He is.....
 A Barney The Bulkhead
 B Mr. Lonely
 C Nowhere Man
 D A Well Respected Man   {51% correct on the Internet}

18. This next guy is something else. He tells lies and makes girls sad. He sends flowers, then goes out with another girl! It seems that it would be best if a girl would stay away from him, for she will never win. He is a.....
   A Secret Agent Man
   B Seventh Son
   C Lifesaver Man
   D Sweet Talkin' Guy   {84% correct on the Internet}

19. Kind of the opposite, we have a mountain of a man who was tall and lean. He carried his Bible in a canvas sack. He was poor but he looked like a king when he rode his horse. Often, he sang the chorus from "Lonesome Valley". He was.....
   A Reverend Mr. Black
   B Tom Dooley
   C Reverend Felcher
   D Old Rivers   {45% correct on the Internet}

20. The last one for this quiz is a "sweet little sixteen". She wears rock 'n' roll shoes, and she checks out Bandstand every day. She only cares about one thing, which is, of course, rock 'n' roll. She even dances to the Yellow Dog Blues! She is.....
   A The Girl From Ipanema
   B Queen Of The Hop
   C Little Bitty Pretty One
   D Rockin' Robin   {55% correct on the Internet}

GAME 8 - MORE GUYS AND GALS

If you liked the previous game.....here's more of the same. If you didn't......oh, well. (There is a 17%-correct-on-the-Internet question in this one.)

1. We start with a young lady from the South, who carried a straight-razor, according to the lyrics. Her mama was working on a chain gang, and the gator's got her granny (for real).....
  A Delta Dawn
  B Lilian Gish
  C Polk Salad Annie
  D Short Fat Fannie   {65% correct on the Internet}

2. The next young lady is in trouble....she wants her mama (who, as far as we know, is not working on a chain gang). She's roaming through the city, going nowhere fast. She's lost and alone, but she made the choice. She's.....
  A Little Jeannie
  B Dirty Diana
  C Pookie
  D Run Away Child, Running Wild   {72% correct on the Internet}

3. This next lady has no one else to use, nobody else to blame. She rode in from another town and she found a fool (and his money), and he says she "better get her face aboard the very next train"....
  A Evil Woman
  B Lizzie Borden
  C Candida
  D Maneater   {67% correct on the Internet}

4. She hypnotizes and she mesmerizes and she should be on Soul Train. She shakes it up, she shakes it down, she moves it in, she moves it around, she is.....
  A Dancing Queen
  B Disco Lady
  C Queen Elizabeth I
  D Lady Marmalade   {63% correct on the Internet}

5. This next young lady is on the flighty side, if you will. She smiles at everyone she sees. She has stormy eyes that "flash at the sound of lies", and sometimes even flies above the clouds! She is.....
   A Stormy
   B Snowy
   C Windy
   D Sunny   {68% correct on the Internet}

6. We'll stay "outdoors" for this one, too. She can get you on "another kind of highway". Her lovin' is the medicine that can save you. She is.....
   A P.T. 109
   B 98.6
   C She's Sexy + 17
   D 25 Or 6 To 4   {56% correct on the Internet}

7. This next young lady is really the cats! She is Mona Lisa with a ponytail. Not only that, the singer thinks that she should be the eighth wonder of the world! She's even a "teenage goddess from above". She is.....
   A Helen Of Troy
   B My True Love
   C Poetry In Motion
   D Venus In Blue Jeans   {75% correct on the Internet}

8. This next girl was was one of those sad stories in song. She was going to be a star, but her name never went up high on the silver screen, in spite of all her efforts. Sadly, like Patches, she killed herself while filled with despair.....
   A Emma
   B Hazel
   C Angie Baby
   D Babe   {17% correct on the Internet}

9. Another female.....it goes on and on. When this one was just a kid, her clothes were hand-me-downs. And "they" laughed at her when she came into town. Yes, she has such a pretty face, she should be dressed in lace. She survived it all, as.....

A Lydia Crosswaithe
B Patches
C Rag Doll
D Bony Maronie   {83% correct on the Internet}

10. Wait.....hold on.....it's a guy. He was born on a summer day in 1951. He was taught how to fight to be nobody's fool. He left home in the winter of 1969, looking for love. He is the.....
A Stranger On The Shore
B Lonesome Loser
C King Of Swing
D Lonely Boy   {55% correct on the Internet}

11. Back to the girls. This one is a "midnight fantasy", just a dream. But, she let him know that there was a love for him out there, somewhere. He was to look for her when he looked in his new-found lover's eyes. She said, "ooo, ooo, ooo-eee". She is.....
A Undercover Angel
B Pam Ewing
C Dream Lover
D Spooky   {61% correct on the Internet}

12. Time for another guy. He is out to get you (if you are a girl, that is). Actually, you could find him anywhere, on a bus or in a grocery store. He is looking for something to happen, like finding someone "to sock it to". We know he drinks coffee and tea.....
A Mr. Big Stuff
B The Old Persuader
C The Rapper
D Midnight Cowboy   {42% correct on the Internet}

13. The Bobbettes, a junior-high female doo-wop group of the 50s, wrote and sang this song about a teacher they actually disliked....
A Mr. Chips
B Mr. Lee
C Old Rivers
D Seymour Skinner   {59% correct on the Internet}

14. It is back to the ladies. She relies on "the old man's money", but it apparently won't get her too far. She needs to know that it's easy to hurt others when she can't feel the pain. This darling is.....
   A Rich Girl
   B American Woman
   C Suzy Creamcheese
   D Lady Blue   {86% correct on the Internet}

15. We can't tell you if this next one is a boy or a girl. We can give some descriptions, though -- never meant to be, born in poverty and always second-best. We're talking shame and guilt here.....
   A Children Of The Night
   B Love Child
   C Baby Love
   D My Girl Bill   {86% correct on the Internet}

16. This one is a young lady. You see, he wouldn't live without her (even if he could?). She is the same little girl who used to hang around his door, but she sure looks different from the way she looked before. He calls her.....
   A Beth
   B Mony Mony
   C Mother Goose
   D Valleri   {64% correct on the Internet}

17. The next one is a "winner". And so many descriptions...she "knows her place", she's got grace, she's never in the way, she's ok alone (no "messin' "). She never asks for much....I guess she is perfect! Oh, yes.....
   A She's About A Mover
   B She's A Lady
   C She's Just My Style
   D She's Shirley   {86% correct on the Internet}

18. Still another female...she has a pretty face that shines on the city nights. She makes the singer feel new...."like a country morning, all smothered in dew". She even feeds him macaroons! She is.....
   A Jackie Blue
   B My Maria

C Sweet City Woman
D The Fat Lady   {68% correct on the Internet}

19. This question is about a woman who has no reason to go home, since she's old enough to "face the dawn". She thinks she may have "sinned", but it's what she wanted, already! She's.....
   A Pocahontas
   B Devil Or Angel
   C Angel Of The Morning
   D Angel Baby   {77% correct on the Internet}

20. For the last one, we have one final "guy question". He works for the county and he needs a small vacation, "but it don't look like rain". He needs her, he wants her. He is the.....
   A Only Law West Of Mt. Pilot
   B Wichita Lineman
   C Ivory Tower
   D Captain Of Her Heart   {76% correct on the Internet}

GAME 9 - FIND THE PHONY (60s)

In this game, one answer is made up (by us). The song titles are the bogus parts, not the artists.

1. We are grooving into the 1960s, and we'll start with place names (remember, you pick the phony title!).....
   A El Paso.....Marty Robbins
   B Ferry Across The Mersey.....Gerry & The Pacemakers
   C Brooklyn Bridge.....Ray Charles
   D Palisades Park.....Freddy Cannon
   E Wolverton Mountain.....Claude King   {57% correct on the Internet}

2. There were a lot of places to go to in the 60s, so we will continue with locations.....
   A Calcutta.....Lawrence Welk
   B Under The Moon.....Elvis Presley
   C Last Train To Clarksville.....The Monkees
   D Memphis.....Lonnie Mack
   E Atlantis.....Donovan   {60% correct on the Internet}

3. Wow! There are lots more, so why stop now.....
   A Galveston.....Glen Campbell
   B Indian Lake.....The Cowsills
   C South Street.....The Orlons
   D North To Alaska.....Johnny Horton
   E Living In L.A......Spirit   {50% correct on the Internet}

4. There are still a lot more, but we will stop going places after this question.....
   A Afternoon In Rio.....Sergio Mendes & Brasil '66
   B Winchester Cathedral.....The New Vaudeville Band
   C Harper Valley P.T.A......Jeannie C. Riley
   D Midnight In Moscow.....Kenny Ball & His Jazzmen
   E Boogaloo Down Broadway.....The Fantastic Johnny C.
                              {33% correct on the Internet}

5. Time to switch. We'll take a break from our journeys and consider some of the more famous "boys" from the 60s.....
   A Beat Nick.....The Jive Five
   B Hey Jude.....The Beatles
   C Speedy Gonzales.....Pat Boone
   D Abraham, Martin And John.....Dion
   E Johnny Angel.....Shelley Fabares   {57% correct on the Internet}

6. Lots of "dudes" made it high on the charts, so we will continue.....
   A Sunshine Superman.....Donovan
   B Matthew.....The Searchers
   C Norman.....Sue Thompson
   D Alley-Oop.....The Hollywood Argyles
   E Simon Says.....1910 Fruitgum Co.   {56% correct on the Internet}

7. Of course, there were many songs with girls names, so.....
   A Hello, Dolly.....Louis Armstrong
   B Dawn (Go Away).....The Four Seasons
   C Sheila.....Tommy Roe
   D Jessica Jones.....The Chi-Lites
   E Patches.....Dickey Lee   {77% correct on the Internet}

8. There are many more "babe" songs, easily enough for one more question.....
   A Runaround Sue.....Dion
   B Hang On Sloopy.....The McCoys
   C I'm Still With Linda.....Everly Brothers
   D Take A Letter Maria.....R.B. Greaves
   E The Ballad Of Bonnie And Clyde.....Georgie Fame   {76% correct on the Internet}

9. Now that you have rested a bit, we'll start traveling again, but this time just to see the animals.....
   A Bee Sting.....The Surfaris
   B Pony Time.....Chubby Checker
   C Pepino The Italian Mouse.....Lou Monte
   D Mockingbird.....Inez and Charlie Foxx
   E Surfin' Bird.....The Trashmen   {42% correct on the Internet}

10. This next question is about animal songs, but only the feline variety.....
   A Nashville Cats.....The Lovin' Spoonful
   B Alley Cat.....Bent Fabric & His Piano
   C What's New, Pussycat?.....Tom Jones
   D The Lion Sleeps Tonight.....The Tokens
   E He's A Tiger.....Mary Wells   {53% correct on the Internet}

11. There were many animal songs in the 60s. We'll do one more, but these will be "animals" someone might have seen after certain questionable activities.....
   A The Unicorn.....The Irish Rovers
   B The Elephant Dance.....Ray Stevens
   C White Rabbit.....Jefferson Airplane
   D Puff The Magic Dragon.....Peter, Paul and Mary
   E Snoopy Vs. The Red Baron.....The Royal Guardsmen
                                           {70% correct on the Internet}

12. The category for the next couple of questions will be colors. In the first one, we'll "go for the green".....
   A Little Green Apples.....O.C. Smith
   B The Ballad Of The Green Berets.....S/Sgt. Barry Sadler
   C Green River.....Creedence Clearwater Revival
   D Green Meadow.....Roger Williams
   E The Jolly Green Giant.....The Kingsmen   {45% correct on the Internet}

13. This question is a mix of "colorful" songs.....
   A White Room.....Cream
   B Lonely Blue Boy.....Conway Twitty
   C Black Nights.....Steppenwolf
   D Deep Purple.....Nino Tempo and April Stevens
   E Red Rubber Ball.....The Cyrkle   {43% correct on the Internet}

14. More colors to choose from.....
   A Black Man, White Man.....Stevie Wonder
   B 1,2,3 Red Light.....1910 Fruitgum Co.
   C Brown Eyed Girl.....Van Morrison

D Paint It, Black.....The Rolling Stones
   E Venus In Blue Jeans.....Jimmy Clanton   {67% correct on the Internet}

15. You know we have to have a couple of love songs, so here we go.....
   A Do You Love Me.....The Contours
   B Everybody Loves Somebody.....Dean Martin
   C To Sir With Love.....Lulu
   D This Guy's In Love With You.....Herb Alpert
   E Take My Love.....Petula Clark   {58% correct on the Internet}

16. 1960s "love" songs seem to be somewhat scarce, but we can get one more question.....
   A Love Is Blue.....Paul Mauriat
   B Love Child.....Diana Ross & The Supremes
   C Will You Love Me Tomorrow.....The Shirelles
   D Love Feels Right.....Percy Sledge
   E Roses Are Red (My Love).....Bobby Vinton   {64% correct on the Internet}

17. Now, we are going to move on to body parts, and the first one is just hearts.....
   A Only Love Can Break A Heart.....Gene Pitney
   B Expressway To Your Heart.....Soul Survivors
   C Wooden Heart.....Joe Dowell
   D The Next Heart.....The Vogues
   E Love Me With All Your Heart.....Ray Charles Singers
                                  {46% correct on the Internet}

18. More body parts, but this one is for your eyes only.....
   A Can't Take My Eyes Off You.....Frankie Valli
   B The Night Has A Thousand Eyes.....Bobby Vee
   C Cryin' Eyes.....Bobby Vinton
   D Pretty Blue Eyes.....Steve Lawrence
   E These Eyes.....The Guess Who   {38% correct on the Internet}

19. Getting near the end, and here is one question about "food" songs.....
   A Sugar, Sugar.....The Archies
   B Incense And Peppermints.....Strawberry Alarm Clock
   C Hot Chocolate.....Sam Cooke
   D Mashed Potato Time.....Dee Dee Sharp
   E Sukiyaki.....Kyu Sakamoto   {66% correct on the Internet}

20. Finally, we end with songs about days of the week, although we just couldn't find any hit songs about Wednesday or Thursday....
   A Pleasant Valley Sunday.....The Monkees
   B Sunday, Sunday.....Dave Clark Five
   C Another Saturday Night.....Sam Cooke
   D Ruby Tuesday.....The Rolling Stones
   E Friday On My Mind.....The Easybeats   {68% correct on the Internet}

GAME 10 - FIND THE PHONY (70s/80s)

This is another game where you have to find a phony song title among the 5 choices.....the artists are real.

1. We'll begin by checking out body parts from the 80s, specifically the "heart part"....
   A Harden My Heart.....Quarterflash
   B Tell Tale Heart.....Olivia Newton-John
   C Owner Of A Lonely Heart.....Yes
   D Total Eclipse Of The Heart.....Bonnie Tyler
   E Queen Of Hearts.....Juice Newton   {83% correct on the Internet}

2. We are staying in the 80s and hopefully you can "see" the bogus answer.....
   A Bette Davis Eyes.....Kim Carnes
   B Eye Of The Tiger.....Survivor
   C Eye In The Sky.....Alan Parsons Project
   D Eye Of The Storm.....Tears For Fears
   E Hungry Eyes.....Eric Carmen   {76% correct on the Internet}

3. We go back a little further on the timeline, into the 70s, and patch together a bunch of body parts.....
   A Hands Up, Give Up.....Isley Brothers
   B Heart of Gold.....Neil Young
   C Smiling Faces Sometimes.....Undisputed Truth
   D Funny Face.....Donna Fargo
   E Sister Golden Hair.....America   {62% correct on the Internet}

4. Still in the 70s, more mixed-up body parts, and a bunch of long titles.....
   A Raindrops Keep Fallin' On My Head.....B.J. Thomas
   B The First Time Ever I Saw Your Face.....Roberta Flack
   C Don't It Make My Brown Eyes Blue.....Crystal Gayle
   D How Can You Mend A Broken Heart.....Bee Gees
   E Feeling Love In My Fingers And My Toes.....The Captain & Tennille   {83% correct on the Internet}

5. Enough with the body parts, already! We'll consider "whole people" now, as you figure out which of these boys from the 80s is a phony.....
   A Mickey.....Tony Basil
   B Luka.....Suzanne Vega
   C Mr. Roboto.....Styx
   D Simply Simon.....Pointer Sisters
   E Jessie's Girl.....Rick Springfield   {84% correct on the Internet}

6. There weren't many boys to pick from in the 80s, but we had a much better selection with the 70s boys.....
   A Jump-Up Johnny .....The O'Jays
   B Freddie's Dead.....Curtis Mayfield
   C Danny's Song.....Anne Murray
   D Fernando.....Abba
   E Amos Moses.....Jerry Reed   {53% correct on the Internet}

7. Let's hear it for the girls, now, and you are looking for an 80s lady that just didn't exist (at least musically).....
   A Angel Anna.....Thompson Twins
   B Gloria.....Laura Branigan
   C Sara.....Starship
   D Elvira.....Oak Ridge Boys
   E Come On, Eileen.....Dexy's Midnight Runners   {79% correct on the Internet}

8. We're just about done with names, but first let's check out the girls of the 70s.....
   A My Sharona.....The Knack
   B Maggie May.....Rod Stewart
   C Honey Bunny.....Nilsson
   D Lay Down Sally.....Eric Clapton
   E Clair.....Gilbert O'Sullivan   {81% correct on the Internet}

9. We are sticking with living creatures, but we're heading to the zoo for the next two. First, from the 80s.....
   A Stray Cat Strut.....Stray Cats
   B Eye Of The Tiger.....Survivor
   C Bat Out Of Hell.....Def Leppard

D Union Of The Snake.....Duran Duran
   E Buffalo Stance.....Neneh Cherry   {65% correct on the Internet}

10. More creatures, only this time from the 70s.....
   A Hummingbird.....Seals and Crofts
   B The Dog.....Honey Cone
   C Disco Duck.....Rick Dees & His Cast of Idiots
   D Dead Skunk.....Loudon Wainwright III
   E Spiders & Snakes.....Jim Stafford   {60% correct on the Internet}

11. There are quite a few songs with places in the title, and the next question has to do with places from the 80s.....
   A Africa.....Toto
   B Key Largo.....Bertie Higgins
   C Kokomo.....Beach Boys
   D Down Under.....Men At Work
   E Alabama.....Kenny Rogers   {67% correct on the Internet}

12. More places, but this time where we went (or didn't go) in the 70s.....
   A Macarthur Park.....Donna Summer
   B Baker Street.....Gerry Rafferty
   C Cincinnati.....Commodores
   D Indiana Wants Me.....R. Dean Taylor
   E Never Been To Spain.....3 Dog Night   {64% correct on the Internet}

13. For the next two questions, we will try colors, with songs from the 80s.....
   A The Lady In Red.....Chris DeBurgh
   B Purple Rose.....INXS
   C Red Red Wine.....UB40
   D Little Red Corvette.....Prince
   E Ebony and Ivory.....Paul McCartney and Stevie Wonder
                              {88% correct on the Internet}

14. More colorful songs, from the 70s this time.....
   A Nights In White Satin.....Moody Blues
   B Goodbye Yellow Brick Road.....Elton John

C Black Water.....Doobie Brothers
   D Yellow High Heels.....Donna Summer
   E Brown Sugar.....Rolling Stones   {89% correct on the Internet}

15. We can't go through this whole exercise without including love songs, of course. First from the 80s.....
    A Endless Love.....Diana Ross and Lionel Ritchie
    B Crazy Little Thing Called Love.....Queen
    C I Love A Rainy Night.....Eddie Rabbitt
    D I've Had It With Love.....Bonnie Tyler
    E The Power Of Love.....Huey Lewis & The News   {90% correct on the Internet}

16. More love songs from the 70s.....
    A Memories Of Your Love.....Peaches and Herb
    B How Deep Is Your Love.....Bee Gees
    C I Think I Love You.....Partridge Family
    D Silly Love Songs.....Wings
    E Come And Get Your Love.....Redbone   {74% correct on the Internet}

17. We are rockin' and rollin' now , once again first from the 80s.....
    A I Love Rock 'N Roll.....Joan Jett & The Blackhearts
    B It's Still Rock And Roll To Me.....Billy Joel
    C Rock With You.....Michael Jackson
    D Rock Me Amadeus.....Falco
    E Rock Rules.....Van Halen   {81% correct on the Internet}

18. More rock 'n' roll, this time from the 70s.....
    A Rock Me Gently.....Andy Kim
    B Rock On.....David Essex
    C Crocodile Rock.....Elton John
    D We Will Rock You.....Queen
    E Heaven Is Rock 'N Roll.....Donny Osmond   {86% correct on the Internet}

19. The next question is about food, songs from the 80s and 70s.....
   A American Pie.....Don McLean
   B Lady Marmalade.....Labelle
   C Lavender Lollipops.....Queen
   D Sukiyaki.....A Taste of Honey
   E One Bad Apple.....Osmonds   {76% correct on the Internet}

20. Lastly, here are some songs about the days of the week, also from both the 70s and 80s (we still couldn't find any hits about Wednesday or Thursday).....
   A Manic Monday.....Bangles
   B Suddenly Sunday.....David Cassidy
   C Saturday Night.....Bay City Rollers
   D Rainy Days And Mondays.....Carpenters
   E New Moon On Monday.....Duran Duran   {63% correct on the Internet}

ANSWERS

Chapter 1 - The 50s and the Early 60s

GAME 1 - ELVIS AND THE EARLY ROCKERS
1 B 2 D 3 A 4 C 5 C 6 D 7 C 8 A 9 B 10 A 11 C 12 D 13 B 14 D 15 B 16 B 17 A 18 C 19 C 20 C

GAME 2 - FLOATIN' THROUGH THE 50s
1 C 2 A 3 B 4 A 5 D 6 D 7 A 8 B 9 B 10 C 11 A 12 C 13 D 14 D 15 D 16 C 17 A 18 B 19 D 20 D

GAME 3 - WHO SANG THESE? (50s/60s)
1 C 2 A 3 A 4 D 5 B 6 C 7 C 8 D 9 D 10 D 11 B 12 A 13 D 14 B 15 C 16 D 17 C 18 A 19 A 20 C

GAME 4 - SUBTITLES FROM THE 50s/60s
1 D 2 B 3 C 4 D 5 A 6 C 7 C 8 A 9 C 10 D 11 B 12 B 13 D 14 A 15 A 16 C 17 D 18 B 19 D 20 C

GAME 5 - SAILIN' THROUGH THE 60s
1 D 2 C 3 C 4 A 5 A 6 D 7 D 8 B 9 A 10 C 11 B 12 C 13 A 14 C 15 D 16 A 17 C 18 A 19 C 20 D

GAME 6 - SARCASTIC 60s
1 B 2 D 3 A 4 D 5 E 6 B 7 A 8 B 9 B 10 E 11 C 12 C 13 E 14 B 15 B 16 A 17 A 18 D 19 E 20 B

GAME 7 - MORE SARCASTIC 60s
1 D 2 B 3 C 4 A 5 B 6 A 7 C 8 C 9 B 10 B 11 B 12 C 13 A 14 C 15 B 16 C 17 C 18 D 19 A 20 B

GAME 8 - WHO SANG THESE? (60s)
1 B 2 A 3 D 4 C 5 D 6 D 7 B 8 A 9 D 10 C 11 C 12 B 13 A 14 D 15 A 16 C 17 D 18 D 19 A 20 B

GAME 9 - THE TRICKY 60s
1 B 2 E 3 C 4 C 5 B 6 C 7 D 8 A 9 E 10 C 11 D 12 B 13 B 14 A 15 C 16 C 17 E 18 D 19 C 20 C

GAME 10 - THE PSYCHEDELIC 60s
1 D 2 B 3 A 4 B 5 A 6 C 7 D 8 A 9 D 10 B 11 C 12 C 13 C 14 A 15 B 16 D 17 C 18 B 19 C 20 B

Chapter 2 - From the 60s to the 70s

GAME 1 - LYRICAL BITS FROM THE 60s AND 70s
1 C 2 D 3 C 4 C 5 A 6 B 7 C 8 C 9 A 10 D 11 B 12 E 13 B 14 A 15 C 16 A 17 A 18 D 19 E 20 D

GAME 2 - 70s WHO - WHAT - WHERE
1 E 2 B 3 A 4 D 5 C 6 A 7 B 8 E 9 A 10 C 11 C 12 D 13 E 14 B 15 A 16 A 17 E 18 C 19 C 20 D

GAME 3 - BITS & PIECES FROM THE 60s AND 70s
1 D 2 A 3 C 4 D 5 C 6 E 7 D 8 D 9 A 10 A 11 C 12 C 13 A 14 C 15 B 16 C 17 C 18 C 19 B 20 A

GAME 4 - BEATLES I
1 D 2 B 3 A 4 C 5 C 6 D 7 A 8 C 9 A 10 A 11 E 12 D 13 B 14 B 15 B 16 A 17 C 18 D 19 E 20 C

GAME 5 - BEATLES II
1 D 2 C 3 D 4 D 5 A 6 D 7 D 8 C 9 D 10 B 11 D 12 A 13 C 14 C 15 B 16 B 17 C 18 D 19 C 20 A

GAME 6 - 60s SOUL
1 C 2 B 3 D 4 A 5 B 6 D 7 B 8 B 9 C 10 A 11 D 12 C 13 A 14 C 15 B 16 A 17 B 18 C 19 C 20 B

GAME 7 - TOUGH SOUL (60s/70s)
1 B 2 D 3 C 4 C 5 D 6 D 7 B 8 B 9 A 10 B 11 B 12 D 13 D 14 C 15 D 16 D 17 A 18 A 19 C 20 B

GAME 8 - QUICKIES FROM THE 60s AND 70s
1 D 2 B 3 A 4 C 5 D 6 D 7 A 8 C 9 D 10 A 11 A 12 B 13 C 14 A 15 C 16 C 17 D 18 C 19 A 20 A

GAME 9 - WHO-WHAT-WHERE IN THE 60s AND 70s
1 C 2 B 3 D 4 D 5 B 6 B 7 A 8 D 9 B 10 A 11 C 12 D 13 E 14 D 15 C 16 B 17 D 18 A 19 E 20 B

GAME 10 - MORE QUICKIES FROM THE 60s AND 70s
1 B 2 D 3 B 4 A 5 E 6 D 7 A 8 D 9 D 10 B 11 D 12 A 13 E 14 C 15 D 16 D 17 A 18 D 19 C 20 C

Chapter 3 - The 70s

GAME 1 - SLIPPIN' THROUGH THE 70s
1 B 2 C 3 A 4 D 5 C 6 B 7 C 8 A 9 D 10 C 11 A 12 C 13 C 14 D 15 D 16 D 17 A 18 B 19 A 20 C

GAME 2 - WHO SANG THESE? (70s)
1 B 2 E 3 D 4 C 5 E 6 D 7 B 8 C 9 A 10 B 11 E 12 D 13 A 14 A 15 E 16 C 17 D 18 B 19 C 20 C

GAME 3 - FLASHBACKS FROM THE 70s
1 E 2 C 3 B 4 A 5 B 6 B 7 E 8 C 9 A 10 E 11 B 12 B 13 E 14 B 15 C 16 C 17 B 18 A 19 B 20 D

GAME 4 - SLIDIN' THROUGH THE 70s
1 C 2 A 3 B 4 D 5 D 6 C 7 B 8 A 9 C 10 D 11 A 12 A 13 A 14 B 15 B 16 D 17 D 18 C 19 C 20 C

GAME 5 - 70s SONG THEMES
1 C 2 A 3 C 4 C 5 D 6 C 7 B 8 D 9 B 10 A 11 D 12 C 13 A 14 C 15 C 16 E 17 C 18 A 19 B 20 D

GAME 6 - MORE 70s SONG THEMES
1 B 2 A 3 C 4 A 5 A 6 C 7 B 8 B 9 B 10 D 11 D 12 D 13 E 14 E 15 A 16 A 17 C 18 B 19 B 20 D

GAME 7 - SUBTITLES FROM THE 70s
1 C 2 A 3 B 4 B 5 C 6 C 7 B 8 D 9 C 10 D 11 A 12 C 13 D 14 D 15 A 16 D 17 C 18 B 19 D 20 C

GAME 8 - WHAT 70s SONG WAS THAT?
1 E 2 A 3 C 4 D 5 A 6 C 7 A 8 D 9 B 10 B 11 B 12 A 13 A 14 C 15 D 16 D 17 B 18 C 19 A 20 E

GAME 9 - 70s VARIETY
1 C 2 C 3 D 4 A 5 C 6 E 7 D 8 D 9 D 10 C 11 A 12 D 13 C 14 A 15 C 16 D 17 B 18 D 19 C 20 B

GAME 10 - THE SNEAKY 70s
1 C 2 C 3 B 4 A 5 A 6 C 7 B 8 B 9 C 10 A 11 A 12 C 13 B 14 B 15 B 16 C 17 A 18 C 19 B 20 C

Chapter 4 - The 80s and the 90s

GAME 1 - 80s SONG THEMES
1 C 2 E 3 B 4 E 5 E 6 C 7 D 8 C 9 A 10 E 11 E 12 D 13 C 14 E 15 D 16 D 17 E 18 A 19 C 20 E

GAME 2 - EASY 80s
1 C 2 B 3 D 4 A 5 A 6 C 7 C 8 C 9 D 10 B 11 C 12 A 13 C 14 D 15 B 16 A 17 B 18 D 19 C 20 C

GAME 3 - MATCH THE LYRICS WITH THE 80s SONG
1 D 2 C 3 A 4 D 5 D 6 C 7 B 8 C 9 A 10 D 11 A 12 D 13 D 14 D 15 D 16 A 17 B 18 C 19 C 20 B

GAME 4 - WHO SANG THESE? (80s)
1 E 2 C 3 B 4 A 5 C 6 B 7 D 8 D 9 A 10 E 11 D 12 B 13 B 14 C 15 A 16 E 17 B 18 E 19 E 20 E

GAME 5 - EYEING THE 80s
1 B 2 B 3 D 4 A 5 B 6 C 7 A 8 D 9 C 10 A 11 A 12 C 13 B 14 D 15 B 16 A 17 C 18 B 19 C 20 A

GAME 6 - MORE 80s
1 A 2 C 3 B 4 B 5 C 6 A 7 C 8 C 9 B 10 A 11 E 12 B 13 C 14 E 15 C 16 D 17 C 18 C 19 A 20 D

GAME 7 - EASIN' THROUGH THE 80s
1 D 2 B 3 A 4 B 5 C 6 C 7 A 8 A 9 D 10 B 11 B 12 C 13 A 14 C 15 D 16 D 17 B 18 A 19 B 20 B

GAME 8 - FLASHBACKS FROM THE 80s
1 C 2 E 3 B 4 E 5 C 6 B 7 A 8 C 9 B 10 B 11 C 12 C 13 C 14 E 15 D 16 B 17 A 18 D 19 A 20 B

GAME 9 - SUBTITLES FROM THE 80s/90s
1 D 2 B 3 C 4 D 5 C 6 A 7 A 8 D 9 C 10 B 11 C 12 B 13 B 14 D 15 B 16 C 17 A 18 A 19 C 20 D

GAME 10 - NAVIGATING THROUGH THE 90s
1 C 2 A 3 C 4 A 5 B 6 B 7 D 8 C 9 C 10 D 11 A 12 C 13 C 14 D 15 C 16 A 17 D 18 C 19 A 20 B

Chapter 5 - Potpourri

GAME 1 - MEMORABLE QUOTES
1 B 2 A 3 D 4 D 5 D 6 D 7 B 8 D 9 B 10 A 11 A 12 C 13 E 14 B 15 C 16 C 17 D 18 C 19 A 20 C

GAME 2 - SILLY SONGS
1 C 2 B 3 D 4 B 5 C 6 A 7 B 8 A 9 D 10 C 11 B 12 A 13 B 14 D 15 A 16 D 17 C 18 C 19 C 20B

GAME 3 - Pretitles THROUGH THE YEARS
1 C 2 B 3 C 4 A 5 B 6 A 7 A 8 C 9 B 10 C 11 C 12 A 13 B 14 B 15 B 16 A 17 C 18 A 19 C 20 A

GAME 4 - ONE-HIT WONDERS
1 B 2 B 3 C 4 D 5 A 6 B 7 E 8 A 9 C 10 E 11 B 12 D 13 A 14 C 15 D 16 A 17 C 18 D 19 D 20 C

GAME 5 - JAMMIN' WITH THE JACKSONS
1 B 2 D 3 D 4 A 5 C 6 A 7 B 8 D 9 C 10 A 11 B 12 A 13 C 14 D 15 D 16 A 17 D 18 C 19 B 20 A

GAME 6 - THE BRITISH INVASION
1 C 2 B 3 A 4 D 5 B 6 C 7 A 8 D 9 C 10 B 11 C 12 C 13 D 14 B 15 A 16 C 17 A 18 C 19 A 20 D

GAME 7 - GUYS AND GALS
1 B 2 D 3 B 4 A 5 C 6 A 7 D 8 C 9 C 10 B 11 D 12 C 13 A 14 B 15 B 16 C 17 D 18 D 19 A 20 B

GAME 8 - MORE GUYS AND GALS
1 C 2 D 3 A 4 B 5 C 6 B 7 D 8 A 9 C 10 D 11 A 12 C 13 B 14 A 15 B 16 D 17 B 18 C 19 C 20 B

GAME 9 - FIND THE PHONY (60s)
1 C 2 B 3 E 4 A 5 A 6 B 7 D 8 C 9 A 10 E 11 B 12 D 13 C 14 A 15 E 16 D 17 D 18 C 19 C 20 C

GAME 10 - FIND THE PHONY (70s/80s)
1 B 2 D 3 A 4 E 5 D 6 A 7 A 8 C 9 C 10 B 11 E 12 C 13 B 14 D 15 D 16 A 17 E 18 E 19 C 20 B

Did you like the book? Do you want to share the experience with others? Wouldn't it make a great gift? For any reason at all, we make it easy to get one or more copies. Just go to *musictriviabook.com* to order what you need. Rock on!

Made in the USA
Lexington, KY
06 April 2017